Mathematicians Are People, Too

Stories from the Lives of Great Mathematicians

◆

Luetta Reimer

Wilbert Reimer

DALE SEYMOUR PUBLICATIONS

To Elaine and Paul

Cover design: Rachel Gage

Order number DS01032
ISBN 0-86651-509-7

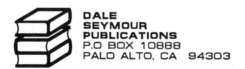

DALE
SEYMOUR
PUBLICATIONS
P.O BOX 10888
PALO ALTO, CA 94303

6 7 8 9 10 11 12-MA-95 94 93

Contents

Introduction and Suggestions for Teachers   iv

Introduction for Students   vi

Pyramids, Olives, and Donkeys ◆ *Thales*   1

The Teacher Who Paid His Student ◆ *Pythagoras*   9

The Man Who Concentrated Too Hard ◆ *Archimedes*   19

A Woman of Courage ◆ *Hypatia*   29

Magician or Mathematician? ◆ *John Napier*   37

Seeing Isn't Believing ◆ *Galileo Galilei*   45

Count on Pascal ◆ *Blaise Pascal*   53

The Short Giant ◆ *Isaac Newton*   63

The Blind Man Who Could See ◆ *Leonhard Euler*   73

The Professor Who Did Not Know ◆ *Joseph Louis Lagrange*   83

Mathematics at Midnight ◆ *Sophie Germain*   91

The Teacher Who Learned a Lesson ◆ *Carl Friedrich Gauss*   99

"Don't Let My Life Be Wasted!" ◆ *Evariste Galois*   107

Life on an Obstacle Course ◆' *Emmy Noether*   115

Numbers Were His Greatest Treasure ◆ *Srinivasa Ramanujan*   123

Resource List   133

Glossary   137

Introduction and Suggestions
for Teachers

◆

Everyone loves a good story. That's why stories are such powerful teaching tools. Behind every mathematical discovery there is a story, often a fascinating one. These stories have rarely been told—yet they are an important part of our heritage, a vital link to our past and a bridge to our future. We hope that this collection will stimulate interest in mathematics by illuminating the people behind the discoveries.

In our increasingly technological world, we need to remember that mathematics is essentially a human endeavor. From these stories, students will discover that mathematics has intrigued both men and women from all cultures since ancient times. Perhaps the stories will help mathematics seem more approachable to some students. One or two may even get "hooked," and find themselves in some future anthology of great mathematicians!

The stories in this book may be used in many ways. You may simply read them aloud to your classes to enrich the mathematics curriculum. Reading one story every week or two would provide an excellent introduction to the history of mathematics. You may also use the stories to introduce mathematical concepts. Hearing how Napier constructed his famous rods, for instance, could lead to the students creating or using the rods to multiply. A study of the metric system might include the story of Lagrange's work. A list of mathematical topics and the stories that feature them is included here for your use.

Because the collection contains nearly one hundred easy-to-understand anecdotes, you might also read the stories in advance and retell pertinent sections in your own words. The anecdotes have an almost magical power to stimulate interest and motivation. They should be part of every mathematics teacher's repertoire.

Students may also read these stories on their own or in small groups, in or out of the classroom. Each story is self-contained and can be read in a short time. Since the stories are not complete biographies, you might encourage students to do additional research on the mathematicians or their work.

Here is a list of mathematical topics and the stories that feature them:

Problem solving: All stories. See especially *Thales, Archimedes, Galileo, Pascal, Newton, Gauss*

Geometry: *Thales, Pythagoras, Archimedes, Pascal, Euler, Gauss*

Number systems and number theory: *Pythagoras, Archimedes, Pascal, Lagrange, Germain, Gauss, Galois, Ramanujan*

Algebra: *Hypatia, Newton, Galois, Noether*

Computation and estimation: *Archimedes, Napier, Pascal, Gauss, Ramanujan*

Probability and statistics: *Pascal*

Women in mathematics: *Hypatia, Germain, Noether*

Measurement: *Thales, Lagrange*

Mathematical symbols: *Napier, Euler*

Introduction for Students

◆

Did you know that Isaac Newton was inspired to study mathematics after a fight with the school bully? Evariste Galois was killed in a duel at age twenty-one, yet his discoveries are still used by mathematicians today. Leonhard Euler wrote more mathematics than anyone—even after he became totally blind. Sophie Germain had to disobey her parents to study mathematics, and Blaise Pascal made one of his most important discoveries because of a toothache!

Mathematicians are people, too! The stories in this book are true stories about real people. Some of the conversations and situations are dramatized—of course nobody knows what Hypatia and her father said to each other, and they certainly weren't speaking English. But from what we know about them, we have tried to re-create a conversation they might have had. Sometimes their words are authentic, taken from letters or other sources.

As you read these stories, notice how these mathematicians solved problems. Note the ways they observed patterns. See how they experimented and tested their observations for accuracy. People use the same techniques to solve problems today.

You could read this entire book in one sitting, but it might be more enjoyable to read one story at a time—or even part of a story. The stories don't include everything known about these mathematicians, so if you're especially interested in one of them, visit your library for more information.

Remember that great mathematical discoveries are made by real people—imperfect people who face the same challenges other people face, including misunderstanding, loneliness, frustration, and physical handicaps. We can learn a lot from them. Their stories show us how they became fascinated with mathematics and how they succeeded through determination and hard work. Most of all, they show us that people achieve great things by doing what they love to do—in spite of the odds against them.

THALES *(THAY-leez)* of **Miletus** *(c.* 636–*c.* 546 B.C.), one of the "Seven Wise Men" of antiquity, was the first known Greek philosopher and scientist. He is the first person with whom the use of deductive methods in mathematics is associated.

Pyramids, Olives, and Donkeys

"To your left you will see the great desert of Giza, and on your right, the three most magnificent pyramids in all of Egypt."

The two Greek travelers squinted in the hot desert sun, awestruck at the tremendous sight before them. The largest pyramid, the Cheops, covered twelve acres.

"You will be interested to know," continued the guide, "that at its base this pyramid measures 518 cubits on each side."

Thales of Miletus was fascinated, and so was his companion. In all their travels throughout Babylon and Egypt, they had seen nothing as grand as the Cheops. The giant white pyramid stood out against the brilliant blue sky. Craning his neck to scan the top of the mighty monument, Thales asked the guide a question.

"How high is this pyramid?"

"I . . . I don't know, sir," the guide responded.

"Well, could you find out for me?"

"Yes, sir; I mean, no, sir. No one knows. This pyramid was built more than 2,000 years ago, and I am only 19 years old."

The flustered guide rushed off to ask his superior what to do about this curious Greek. Soon a small group of guides were huddled together, arguing and shouting. After all, some argued, it was impossible to measure the height of the Cheops. Even if someone could get to the top and throw down a rope, that would only measure the slant, not the height.

"Young man! Guide!" shouted Thales. "Never mind my question. I've figured it out. In case anyone else asks, the top of the pyramid is 329 cubits high."

The guides stopped arguing and their mouths hung open. They fell down on the ground, assuming that Thales was a powerful magician. Who knew what would happen next?

During these times, about 600 B.C., people used superstition or mythology to explain most natural processes. The guides would never have believed that Thales had used simple observation and a little geometry to determine the pyramid's height. But that's exactly what he did.

Thales and his friend had been walking around the pyramid when suddenly Thales noticed the pyramid's shadow. Like his own shadow, it kept changing as the sun dropped lower in the sky. But each shadow changed in proportion, and that gave him the clue he needed. Thales knew his height and his shadow's height. He also knew the height of the pyramid's shadow. The missing information was the pyramid's height. Since he had three of the four numbers he needed for a proportion, Thales could figure out the missing number:

$$\frac{Height\ of\ Thales}{Height\ of\ Thales's\ shadow} = \frac{Height\ of\ pyramid\ \textbf{(unknown)}}{Height\ of\ pyramid's\ shadow}$$

News about Thales's discovery spread quickly throughout Egypt. Everyone was astonished at his cleverness. But solving problems was an old hobby for Thales. In Miletus, where he grew up and became known as a successful merchant, the street corners were always buzzing with a new story of Thales's adventures.

"What do you think of this new idea of using coins for trade, Thales?" asked a merchant friend one day.

"I think it's a fine idea, Milo. It probably will improve business tremendously."

"Humph! Coins might make it easier to *do* business, but that doesn't mean there will be *more* business. It seems that I just can't get ahead. The poor man doesn't have a chance in this world."

"Nonsense, Milo. Anyone with a little money to invest can make a fortune—you just have to use your head."

"Humph! You think you're so smart, Thales. Why don't you prove it for a change?" Milo challenged. "I'm going away for half a year. When I come back, you show me your riches."

"Agreed," said Thales. "I will wait for you dressed in the finest linen and jewels."

Thales set right to work, looking for a way to make his fortune. Soon he observed that one of the Greek economy's chief resources was in decline. The people used olive oil to make soap, fuel lamps, cook, and soften their skin. But for several years, the small, gnarled trees that dotted the landscape had not produced olives. Thales studied the orchards. He noted the weather cycles of the previous three or four years. He talked to old-timers who had seen this happen before. And he discovered a pattern.

Soon Thales was scurrying about the community, offering to buy an olive oil press from everyone who had one. Of course people were eager to sell. Who wanted a useless old contraption cluttering up the yard?

By the time the trees bloomed and olives began to ripen, Thales owned all the presses in the community. Exactly as he had predicted, there was a bumper crop of olives. The trees were studded with the pungent black fruit, and Thales made a fortune renting out presses to his fellow citizens. When the harvest ended, he had enough money to travel to Egypt, with plenty left over to impress Milo. But Thales wasn't really interested in the money. After the harvest, he sold all the presses back at a fair price and, to poorer farmers, even gave them back free. His purpose was not to go into the olive oil business, but to show that one can profit from observing patterns and making predictions.

Though he much preferred to travel or study astronomy, sometimes Thales had to work for a living. One source of income was a salt mine he owned in the hills near Miletus. Each day Thales's workers mined the salt and loaded it onto a caravan of donkeys for the trip down the hill to the marketplace. Between the mine and the town the donkeys had to cross a small river. It was not deep or treacherous, but one day a donkey tripped and fell into the water. Several days later when Thales was visiting the mine, his foreman reported on a strange occurrence.

"I'm afraid you'll have to replace Hector, sir. He's just not steady on his feet anymore. Every day when we cross the river, he slips and falls into the water, ruining his load of salt."

"Does he have a leg injury?" Thales wondered aloud. "Is he limping?"

"That's what's so odd, sir. He walks perfectly, uphill and down, until we get to the river. I've had several different men look at him, and no one can find anything wrong."

Thales's head buzzed with the question that always haunted him, even though he didn't care much about donkeys or salt. The question was: *why?*

The next day Thales waited at the river for the donkey train to arrive. He watched each donkey walk carefully through the stream until Hector eased into the water and rolled over onto his back. Before long, he righted himself, shook his head, and picked his way back to the line of donkeys.

"Aha!" shouted Thales. "I see it now! Hector has learned that the water will dissolve his heavy load of salt. If he dips into the river, he's light as a young colt the second half of his journey. He'll never carry salt again, unless I teach him a lesson."

The next day Thales personally loaded Hector. Instead of putting salt into the sacks, he filled them with sponges. At first the load was unusually light for Hector. As usual, he eased into the cool water expecting an even lighter burden. What a surprise for that donkey! The sponges absorbed water from the river, making Hector's load heavier than ever. After several days of this "medicine," Hector was cured of his bad habit.

Thales didn't write this or other stories down in a book or a letter. Aesop and Plato, two other famous Greeks, kept his stories alive by retelling them. Eventually they were collected and written down. Many of Thales's experiences became bedtime stories for Greek children and children around the world. No one is sure if all the stories happened exactly the way they are told, but everyone agrees that Thales was a brilliant and influential man.

In one story, Thales predicted a solar eclipse. In a solar eclipse, the moon comes between the sun and the earth. Because the moon blocks the sun's light, the sky suddenly becomes as dark as night. At this time, eclipses were mysterious and frightening. No one in Greece knew how to predict an eclipse precisely. However, some scholars think Thales had studied solar patterns with the Egyptians and the Chaldeans. He may have used these patterns to forecast the eclipse. When he predicted it, the Medes and Lydians had been at war, stubbornly fighting for six years. They scoffed at Thales's warning of coming darkness—but on May 28, 585 B.C., the world suddenly grew dark in the middle of the day. Both sides were terrified and quickly signed a peace treaty.

Many different adjectives can be used to describe Thales. We can call him inventive, imaginative, resourceful, inquisitive, and brilliant. But the word most often used to describe him is simply "first." Thales was the first of the "Seven Wise Men" of Greece, a list that later Greeks compiled. He was the first philosopher and the first mathematician. He was the first to use deductive reasoning, a type of logic, to solve problems. He was the first to experiment with electricity, rubbing amber to make static. He was the first to suggest that a year was made up of 365 days, instead of 12 months with 30 days each. He was also the first to state the basic theorems of geometry.

In dedicating his life to answering the questions "Why?" and "How?" Thales contributed greatly to the development of science and mathematics. Every time we observe a pattern and predict an outcome, we follow his example.

PYTHAGORAS (*pi-THAG-uh-rus*) **of Samos** (*c.* 560–*c.* 480 B.C.) was a Greek philosopher and religious leader, responsible for important developments in the history of mathematics, astronomy, and the theory of music. Pythagoras is most famous for the theorem on right triangles that bears his name.

The Teacher Who Paid His Student

"**P**sst! Young man! Over here!"

The ragged Greek boy stopped in his tracks. Had he really heard someone calling him from behind that vegetable cart?

"Here! Here I am! Come here. I have an offer for you."

The boy, whose name was Philocrates, bent over to look around the wagon. The eyes he saw peering back at him looked a bit wild, but kind.

"What do you want with me?" answered Philocrates. "Surely you can see that I have no money to buy your wares! I'm just a poor street boy, trying to make a living doing odd jobs for anyone who will hire me."

"I have no wares to sell, except the truth," the stranger said. "Wouldn't you like to learn it?"

Philocrates scratched his head. He had met some unusual people, but this fellow seemed really different. The man's eyes sparkled, and his manner seemed friendly enough. But truth? How could truth fill one's stomach?

"Sorry, friend," he replied. "I have to keep working the streets so that my mother and sisters and I can eat each day. Perhaps you can sell your truth to someone more wealthy than I."

He picked up his roughly woven sack of tools and waved a quick farewell.

"Wait! Please wait," the stranger called. "Let me introduce myself. My name is Pythagoras and I was born here on the island of Samos. But I have traveled to Miletus and Egypt and was even captured and taken to Babylon for seven years. The things I have learned in these travels—oh, my son, you would be thrilled to learn them!"

"I'm sure I would, sir, but you don't understand my problem. I have no money, so I must work. It's that simple."

"All right," Pythagoras offered. "I'll make you a deal. If you will let me teach you, I will pay you what you would normally earn at your other work." He paused to let his unusual proposition sink in. "Well, what do you say? Shall we start tomorrow morning? You can meet me here by this bench."

Something drew Philocrates towards this odd teacher, but his practical nature made him resist. Finally he decided he would give it a try. If the stranger didn't really have any money to pay him for playing student, he could always quit and go back to his odd jobs. What did he have to lose?

"All right. We'll start tomorrow. But remember, I need daily wages."

The next day the strange pair began their first lesson in the alley where they had met, amidst the cries of merchants and the mingled smells of fish, freshly baked honey cakes, and sweating donkeys carrying goods to sell. While the townspeople shopped and gossiped, Pythagoras and his student squatted in the dirt. The eager teacher drew shapes and figures on the ground. To Philocrates, it was all new but intriguing. And, just as he promised, at the end of the day Pythagoras paid.

Day after day it was the same. Each time Philocrates learned a new lesson Pythagoras paid him three oboli, about a penny. Soon he was making far more money than he could have made doing errands and odd jobs. He was an excellent student and quickly built up quite a savings account.

Pythagoras loved the arrangement, too. It was exhilarating to have an eager young mind absorb his ideas. Unfortunately, Philocrates learned so quickly and well that Pythagoras was soon out of money.

"I'm sorry to tell you this, Philocrates, but today will be our last lesson. I have no more money to pay your wages, so you will have to find other ways to support yourself."

"But Pythagoras, you can't quit teaching me now," the boy protested. "I'm just starting to understand arithmetic and you were going to teach me astronomy and geometry, too."

"I'm sorry, young man, but I see no other choice."

Philocrates hung his head and thought. In a moment he came up with an idea.

"I know! You have been paying me to learn; now I will pay you to teach."

So for the next several months the two continued to meet, but this time the student paid the teacher. By the time the lessons were completed, Pythagoras had become an experienced teacher, and

Philocrates had gained an excellent education!

Pythagoras's first "school" with Philocrates may have had only one student. But several years later he founded a real school at Croton, a Greek colony in southern Italy. This school became so influential it changed even the way people thought about knowledge. During his many travels, Pythagoras had gained quite a reputation. Some people even thought he was divine, or the son of their god Apollo. When he called together a group of wealthy scholars to form a school, no wonder many responded enthusiastically.

The students in Pythagoras's school were all adults. He divided them into two grades depending on their knowledge. The first grade was called the *acoustici*, or the listeners. They were invited to listen to Pythagoras lecture but were not allowed to see him—they had not yet proven themselves worthy. He stood behind a curtain, where only the second grade, the *mathematici*, could see him.

After three years of listening to their teacher's voice, the *acoustici* were admitted into the inner circle of learners. Seeing Pythagoras must have been worth waiting for. He had a flair for the dramatic and dressed like a stage performer. While the students waited for Pythagoras's entrance, musicians played popular music. Finally the curtain was drawn back and Pythagoras, stately in his white robe, appeared before the learners. His feet were strapped with gold sandals, and his head was crowned with a golden wreath. No wonder people suspected him of having gods for ancestors.

Pythagoras worked most of his problems in the sand. His classroom always had a good supply of sand on the floor, and his attendants stood by with a selection of differently-colored sand in containers. When Pythagoras wanted to show one part of a geometric shape, for instance, the attendants would fill that part with blue or green sand so that students could see it more easily.

Pythagoras gave lectures on "mathemata," which in his language meant studies of all kinds. Because Pythagoras emphasized arithmetic and geometry, the word came to mean mathematics as we know it today. He also taught astronomy and music, but he believed that everything in the universe depended on numbers. Pythagoras and his followers chose the motto "All is Number." They were convinced that if they understood numbers, they would hold the key to life itself.

Because Pythagoras and his students believed that knowledge was powerful, they wanted to control it. They became secretive about what they knew. The school was a "Secret Brotherhood," and everyone who joined had to promise never to tell outsiders about their discoveries. If anyone did tell, the results could be disastrous for him or her.

"Have you heard about Hippasus?"

The question hummed throughout Croton.

"Yes. Isn't it horrible? Just because he broke the code of the Brotherhood. It doesn't seem fair."

"But the gods are always fair. He knew better than to tell about the discovery of irrational numbers."

"He must have known he would be expelled from Pythagoras's Secret Brotherhood. Do you suppose he thought that would be his only punishment?"

"I don't know. But there's something suspicious about the way he drowned, falling off that boat in such calm weather."

People were always talking about the Secret Brotherhood, also known as the Pythagorean School. Schools of adults were common, but this group had some unusual ideas. They became a kind of religious order with their own set of initiations and rites.

The 300 members of the Brotherhood shared whatever they had with each other. They were unusually kind to animals because they believed that human souls might come back after death for another life in an animal body. They were vegetarian and would not even wear wool because it came from sheep. If they could choose, they always took a low road instead of a high road, to show their humility. They would not poke a fire with iron because fire was the symbol of truth. They would not touch white roosters or eat beans, because both roosters and beans symbolized perfection. On their clothing they each wore their sacred symbol—the pentagram, a five-pointed star.

In one way the Brotherhood was unusually progressive. During Pythagoras's day, women were forbidden to attend public meetings of any kind, but Pythagoras welcomed them to his school. Of course, they had to prove themselves just as the male students did. Nevertheless, at one time the select *mathematici* class included at least 28 women.

Because the Pythagoreans shared everything, it is hard to separate Pythagoras's discoveries from those of his followers. Much of modern mathematics is based on their work. Like Thales before him, Pythagoras insisted on mathematical proof. It was not enough to say that two angles were equal because they looked equal. One had to prove it. Pythagoras is most famous for providing the first logical proof of this theorem:

> *In a right triangle, the square of the hypotenuse is equal to the sum of the squares of the other two sides.*

The common formula for this theorem, if *c* is the length of the hypotenuse and *a* and *b* the lengths of the other two sides, is

$$a^2 + b^2 = c^2.$$

The Pythagoreans were also the first to divide all numbers into even and odd. They learned to construct the five regular solids, the only solids whose faces are all the same shape and size: the tetrahedron (four sides), the cube (six sides), the octahedron (eight sides), the dodecahedron (twelve sides), and the icosahedron (twenty sides). The first two had been known from ancient times, but the others had never been constructed.

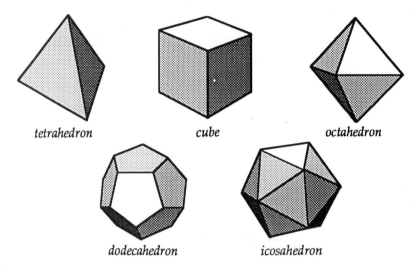

tetrahedron   cube   octahedron

dodecahedron   icosahedron

The Pythagoreans learned to construct the five regular solids.

Great thinkers are not always appreciated in their own times. The Pythagoreans were often misunderstood. Many of their ideas and practices seemed strange to their countrymen. Some towns-people suspected the Pythagoreans would try to take over the local government. They blamed the Pythagoreans, who were quite wealthy, for trying to keep them poor. One day in about 500 B.C., an angry mob set the Pythagoreans' meetinghouse on fire during a lecture. Only a few members survived, and Pythagoras himself was killed. Some say that his students formed a human bridge over the fire so that he could escape—but when he reached a field of beans, he surrendered to his enemies rather than trample the sacred bean plants.

By this time chapters of the Brotherhood had spread throughout Sicily and southern Italy. For many years men and women continued to discuss the ideas Pythagoras had introduced. Today, all students of geometry and higher mathematics work with concepts that Pythagoras discovered. The search for knowledge and truth continued long after Pythagoras's death and the end of the Brotherhood. It continues today wherever people are willing to pursue it.

ARCHIMEDES (*ar-ki-MEE-deez*), 287–212 B.C., was the greatest mathematician of ancient times. He made many original contributions to geometry and laid the foundation for integral calculus. His inventions include the catapult and Archimedes's screw.

The Man Who Concentrated Too Hard

Gleaming and glistening in the sun, the *Syracosia* was so bright the king and all his subjects had to squint to look at her. She sat in the shipyard, waiting to be launched. This was no ordinary ship, that was for certain. The *Syracosia* was crafted of the finest materials and, stern to bow, decked out with the latest in modern devices and luxurious furnishings.

There was just one little problem. In his desire to please and impress King Ptolemy of Alexandria, who had ordered the ship, King Hieron had built it too big. Now that it was finished, there was no way to get it into the water. King Hieron decided to use the tactic that had solved so many of his problems.

"Send for Archimedes!"

Archimedes was never thrilled about having his own work interrupted. However, he *had* boasted to the king once that if he were given someplace to stand he could move the whole earth. This is because Archimedes had discovered the law of the *lever*. By using a lever, people can easily lift objects much heavier than their own weight. It is this law that makes seesaws work. Archimedes's levers could move very heavy objects. Now Hieron wanted him to prove he could move a big ship, and Archimedes looked forward to the challenge.

When he got to the dry dock where the ship had been built, Archimedes was amazed at the crowds gathered there. Columns of workers loaded the ship with cargo. On another ramp, stewards helped passengers onto the decks. Hieron was determined to make the ship as heavy as possible. If he turned the problem into a test of Archimedes's creativity, perhaps he could cover his embarrassment at having built such a monster!

Archimedes went to work. With the help of some young boys who worked for him, he placed a collection of pulleys, levers, and ropes around the base of the ship. Everyone knew that these mechanical devices could never move so great a ship as the *Syracosia*. What did Archimedes think he was going to do with those contraptions?

Finally, everything was ready. Archimedes went to sit in a low chair on the beach. At a signal from Hieron, Archimedes gently tugged on the rope attached to the first pulley. Smoothly, almost effortlessly, the beautiful ship began to move towards the sea. Soon the ship glided into the water, while the puzzled townspeople cheered and scratched their heads.

Archimedes was a great problem solver. He liked to think about scientific problems, such as how to measure the circumference of a circle. However, he was willing to help with the practical problems in his home town, Syracuse. At that time, Syracuse was a part of Greece. Archimedes had been born there as had his father

Pheidias, and he was fond of the city. Situated on the coast of the island of Sicily, Syracuse was rapidly becoming an important trade center. It was also a perfect spot for thinking. Archimedes had gone to Alexandria to study when he was a young man, but even the good friends he met there could not draw him away from Syracuse.

Archimedes's father, Pheidias, had been a noted astronomer. That could be why Archimedes found the sun, the moon, and the planets so fascinating. One day he started thinking about big numbers. Most people believed that the number indicating how many grains of sand filled the seashore didn't exist. The sand couldn't be counted, so the number must be too big to imagine. Archimedes loved a challenge; he set out to count the sand. As if that wasn't hard enough, he decided to count how much sand it would take to fill up the entire known universe. (In those days, people thought the universe was the space between the sun, moon, and the five planets identified at that time—Venus, Mercury, Mars, Jupiter, and Saturn.)

First, Archimedes counted how many grains of sand made up a cluster the size of a poppy seed. Then he counted how many poppy seeds equaled the size of a man's finger. He calculated how many fingers it would take to fill a stadium. Archimedes kept going like this until he came up with his answer: 10^{63} grains.* This number illustrates Archimedes's new system for writing large numbers. He used *exponents* to indicate how many times a number should be multiplied by itself.

Archimedes's estimate of the size of the universe was too small, but he did count how much sand it would take to fill that space.

Read this number as "ten to the 63rd power." Sixty-three is an exponent.

This introduced a new way of thinking about numbers. From then on, no number was too big.

"Archimedes," said King Hieron one day, "I have another problem for you."

"Yes, your Majesty. How can I help?"

"This situation," the king said carefully, "is a bit uncomfortable for me. Will you promise to tell no one of my dilemma?"

"Of course. You know you can trust me."

"Yes, yes. Here is my problem. I have had a new crown crafted by Dionthenes. It's here, wrapped in this velvet cloth."

"It's magnificent, your Highness. Aren't you happy with it?"

"I'm pleased with the way it looks, but something tells me that it isn't quite as I ordered," the king explained. "You see, I took the required amount of gold to Dionthenes's shop and asked him to craft this crown. But now I wonder if the goldsmith substituted silver inside the crown, and kept some of the more valuable gold for himself."

"Hmmm." Archimedes was stumped. "Naturally, you wouldn't want to cut into such a beautiful crown. I suppose you've checked it to see that it weighs the same as the gold you gave Dionthenes?"

King Hieron nodded. He looked a bit forlorn that Archimedes hadn't solved his problem instantly.

Archimedes promised to think about it and wandered off, absent-mindedly talking to himself. He often got so absorbed in problems that he forgot to watch where he was going, bumping into merchants and walking in front of carts. Sometimes he forgot about eating until his friends reminded him.

One day Archimedes was relaxing at the public bath house. As he sat in the tub, an idea struck like lightning. He was so excited about his discovery that he jumped up and ran down the streets shouting "Eureka, eureka!" ("I have found it!"). Archimedes had discovered the natural law of *buoyancy*. However, most people would have remembered to dress before running down the street!

In the bath, Archimedes observed the amount of water displaced by his body. He noticed that the water level rose and fell as he lowered and lifted his weight, and that the water buoyed him up more when his body was completely submerged. The water's *buoyancy* kept him afloat. As he thought about it, he realized that the greater the volume for the water to support, the greater the buoyancy. Large objects—ones with greater volume— are more buoyant than smaller objects of the same weight. For example, a six-inch plastic ruler and a nickel weigh the same, but the ruler floats and the nickel sinks. The ruler has greater volume and is therefore more buoyant because it has more volume for the water to support.

Archimedes knew that the crown Dionthenes designed for King Hieron weighed the same as the gold that the king gave him. But if the crown displaced more water than the gold, that meant its *volume* must be greater, so it must be filled with something less dense than gold—like silver. He put the gold under water and measured how much the water rose. Then he did the same thing with the crown, and the water rose higher—proof that the crown had greater volume and could not be pure gold. The king's suspicions were confirmed. No one knows for sure what happened to the craftsman, but it's not pleasant to imagine.

When he wasn't solving problems for the king, Archimedes was busy at work on his own discoveries. He wrote many pamphlets about his findings. Some of these can be seen in museums today.

Archimedes often conducted studies of the circle. He was determined to find a precise ratio between the *circumference* of a circle and its *diameter*. To do this, he drew a many-sided *polygon* inside a circle and then drew another polygon enclosing the circle. This helped him come up with a remarkably accurate *ratio*. After much experimentation, Archimedes announced that it was less than $3\frac{1}{7}$ and greater than $3\frac{10}{71}$. This ratio, called *pi* (π), has now been calculated to many decimal places.

Archimedes's work on circles led him to study all sorts of curves, spheres, and spirals. He spent much time drawing and making models, carefully writing down his observations. If writing materials were not handy, he spread out cold ashes from the fire and drew in them. Often he worked in the sand. Finally he put together his proofs for finding areas, volumes, and centers of gravity for curves, surfaces, circles, spheres, conics, and spirals. The achievement that Archimedes was proudest of was his discovery of how to calculate the volume of a sphere. He found that it equals two-thirds the volume of the smallest cylinder that will enclose it. He was so proud of this discovery that he requested that the sphere-and-cylinder diagram he worked with be engraved on his tombstone. Archimedes made so much progress in his studies that further work in this area was not possible until new tools were developed eighteen centuries later.

"Have you ever considered how wealthy you could be if you worked on practical things instead of all these figures?" asked one of Archimedes's neighbors one day.

"Perhaps money and fame are important to some. I would rather work at what really interests me," Archimedes responded.

"But you invented the water screw, didn't you? That's practical, isn't it?"

"I suppose everyone must do some things to help others," Archimedes mused, "but I would feel like a failure if I spent my whole life designing mechanical toys."

Compared to his mathematical research, inventions like the water screw seemed like toys to Archimedes. But the water screw was actually an important and practical tool. It was a tube, open at each end, that enclosed a rod. When the lower end was immersed in water at an angle and the upper end was rotated, the screw worked like a straw, drawing the water up and out the top. In Egypt, farmers used this invention to get water out of the Nile River for irrigation. Seamen also used the screw to bail water out of their ships. In Spain the screw was used to pump water out of silver mines being excavated.

Towards the end of his life Archimedes *had* to give more of his time to such practical devices. Sicily, the island of which Syracuse was capital, found itself caught between Rome and Carthage, which were fighting the Punic Wars. After King Hieron died, his grandson Hieronymus took over Sicily and foolishly allied the nation with Carthage. The Romans planned to attack and easily conquer Sicily, but they had not planned on Archimedes's creative weaponry.

Under Archimedes's direction, the military began an aggressive building program. First he showed them how to set up huge catapults, machines that could throw heavy stones over the city walls onto ships in the harbor. Then they built long poles on bases that could be wheeled to any part of the wall. These projected over the wall, and when a lever was released, dropped ship-destroying weights on the enemy below. Archimedes also designed massive cranes that could reach over the wall, pick up a ship, and dump all the sailors on board into the sea.

The Romans tried for two years to capture Syracuse, but without success. After seeing so many of Archimedes's ingenious weapons, some of the Roman sailors were understandably nervous. Sometimes if a ship got too close to the harbor, the Greeks would just hang a loose rope over the wall. The Romans were sure it was another of Archimedes's inventions to destroy them, and would flee in fear for their lives.

The Roman commander Marcellus was frustrated and angry at being defeated by a mathematician. But he was patient. He waited for a day when the Greeks would let down their guard. It happened during a festival honoring Artemis, Greek goddess of the moon. The Syracuse soldiers relaxed and took a holiday, eating and drinking so much they forgot to keep a sharp lookout. Before they knew what had happened, the Romans had conquered the city.

Archimedes had angered Marcellus, but Marcellus respected the mathematician's brilliance and creativity. Before his soldiers left ship, Marcellus gave strict instructions that Archimedes should be captured alive: no harm should come to him.

Unlike his countrymen, Archimedes was not celebrating when the Romans attacked. As usual, he was deeply involved in a problem. He had no idea anything unusual was happening, but he knew someone was standing in the light, making a shadow on the ground where he was drawing his geometric shapes.

"Get out of the light, will you?" he said. "Can't you see I'm working?"

"Rise and follow me, old man!" the soldier commanded.

Archimedes didn't hear him. He kept working, his brow furrowed in deep concentration. He didn't notice the soldier angrily unsheath his sword. Proud and arrogant, the soldier disobeyed Marcellus's order and killed the greatest creative genius of the ancient world.

Marcellus was deeply grieved. He immediately planned an elaborate ceremony to honor Archimedes. He did everything he could to comfort Archimedes's family. And he made sure that, as Archimedes had requested years earlier, a picture of a sphere within a cylinder was engraved on his tombstone.

HYPATIA (*hy-PAY-shuh*), 370–415 A.D., was a brilliant Greek scholar and professor at the University of Alexandria. Known as the first woman mathematician, she advanced the study of algebra and built scientific instruments.

A Woman of Courage

"Are we almost there, Father?" the young girl panted.

"Yes, yes. But reserve some breath for the final climb. I've planned a steep one for today."

"Just lead me to it. I'll leave you in the dust," she teased.

Hypatia and her father, Theon, ran each day in the hills above Alexandria. It was part of their physical fitness routine.

"Here it is," her father announced. "Turn right past that palm and run straight up the knoll."

Hypatia was already winded from the six-mile run, but her father's challenge was enough to spur her on. She darted up the short path and was already resting on a little patch of grass when he arrived.

"Need some help, Father?" she taunted with a grin.

"I'll beat you next time! Don't be too proud. After all, you're just a youngster and I'm an old man." He flung himself down beside her and kiddingly boxed her arm.

It was a perfect morning in Alexandria. From their resting spot they overlooked the city on the Egyptian coast and the Mediterranean Sea beyond. The city glistened under the vivid blue sky.

"Look at that magnificent new sailing ship in port, Father. It must have come in during the night."

"Yes, I see it. Sometimes I think we would be better off without such a powerful lighthouse," Theon replied. "Alexandria is becoming better known as a city of commerce than a city of learning."

"Now don't criticize our lighthouse, Father. I'm honored to live near one of the Seven Wonders of the World."

"You're right, Hypatia. But I can't help remembering how the city first became famous. I long for those days when instead of commercial goods, sailing ships brought the greatest minds in the world to Alexandria," he explained. "In those times the city built museums and libraries. Now, under the Romans, it builds manufacturing and trading centers."

Hypatia mused for a while. Her father's melancholy spirit was contagious. It was true: the passion for learning that she had read about was no longer so evident in Alexandria. But maybe it wasn't completely dead.

"Time changes things, Father," she said. "But look. From here we can see that the city's heart is still the search for learning and truth. The university with its library and museum are clearly at the center of the city. Surely Ptolemy, who helped bring knowledge here 700 years ago, knew that other influences would also come to Alexandria. The same qualities that made it perfect for learning make it perfect for commerce."

"I know you are right, Hypatia," Theon admitted. "I just wish the Romans had more sympathy for thinking and inquiry. In mathematics especially, they have no taste for anything that they can't use to win battles or make money."

"Now you're starting to sound like a mathematics professor!" his daughter laughed.

Indeed, Theon was a mathematics professor, and a very good one. Since her mother had died when she was a baby, Hypatia spent most of her time with her father, either at the university or exploring Alexandria. When she was very young, Hypatia demonstrated unusual intelligence. Theon determined to help her become as close to perfect as possible. Besides teaching her everything he knew, he provided her with formal training in the arts, literature, science, and philosophy. He believed that the body as well as the mind could be perfected. He set up a carefully-planned regimen of exercise and diet and personally trained with Hypatia. With Theon to teach her, tutor her, and play with her, learning and growing was hard work, but fun too.

The results were spectacular. By the time Hypatia was a young woman, she was both brilliant and beautiful. People came from around the world to listen to her teach. She was so eloquent and so strikingly beautiful, some of her students thought she was an oracle—a wise person whose knowledge came from the gods.

Hypatia traveled much more than most people did. She thrived on studying other cultures. For a while, she attended a school taught by Plutarch and his daughter Asclepigenia in Athens, Greece. When she returned to Alexandria the university offered her a teaching position, where she taught with other celebrated scholars. For students and visitors, Hypatia's lecture room and her home were two favorite spots.

Besides teaching, Hypatia wrote a series of mathematical treatises, or scholarly articles, that she used to teach her students. Some of the current mathematics books were difficult to understand, so Hypatia wrote notes explaining their ideas more clearly.

Occasionally, she advised other mathematicians and scientists through letters. Much of the information about Hypatia comes from her letters to Synesius of Cyrene, Greece, who later became an important philosopher. Synesius was having trouble collecting information for some experiments. Hypatia suggested he could make the measurements he needed using equipment she had designed: an *astrolabe*, which measured the positions of stars and planets, and a *planisphere*, another device used for studying astronomy. She also invented a device to distill water and measure its properties.

But Hypatia was not only a well-known scientist and mathematician; she also became a highly respected philosopher. Her father had taught her to be open-minded about ideas. Like many Greeks, he believed people should keep questioning rather than settle on one version of truth as final. He introduced her to a variety of religions, and she learned to value the good in each. Because of this, she taught her students to ask lots of questions, even about ideas that government or religious leaders said they should not question. Eventually, this caused trouble for Hypatia.

Hypatia got caught in the middle of a struggle between two leaders in Alexandria. Orestes, *prefect* or governor of Alexandria, was Hypatia's friend. They enjoyed talking together and often wrote letters about the latest ideas. Cyril was the archbishop of Alexandria, the head of the Christian church in that city. He was suspicious of anyone who did not accept his religious views. Conflict developed between the two men and their followers, and Cyril became convinced that Hypatia was behind it.

Early one morning Orestes paid a surprise visit to Hypatia's home. "I must talk to you immediately," he whispered.

Hypatia was alarmed. Orestes was usually so calm and controlled. Now he was out of breath and his forehead was furrowed with worry. "What is it?" she asked, her eyes wide with surprise.

"We must never see each other again," Orestes said, his voice low. "And we must not write to each other or even send messages. It has become too dangerous."

"What do you mean, Orestes? It is a sad world we live in when two persons cannot think together."

"Cyril is making threats again," Orestes explained. "I fear for your safety."

"I don't fear Cyril," Hypatia said. "His threats are just for show. Surely he would never actually harm anyone."

"I used to agree with you, Hypatia, but now I am persuaded that Cyril means business." He paused a moment and looked at the floor. "You haven't heard about what happened during the night?"

"No, I don't know what you're talking about."

"Cyril's men set fire to the library, Hypatia. Most of the precious scrolls are gone."

Hypatia was stunned. She thought of her father and the years he had dedicated to learning and teaching in Alexandria. She thought of all the other men and women who had spent their lives building the library and the university. After a long time, she bit her lip and spoke. "Orestes, the lighthouse of Alexandria may be shining, but the true light of our city is being extinguished."

After several months of skirmishes and squabbles between Orestes's and Cyril's followers, Cyril decided to show his power in an unforgettably cruel act. He ordered that Hypatia be murdered.

An angry mob of religious fanatics, fired up by false rumors of Hypatia's teachings, kidnapped her one day as she rode through town on her chariot. They dragged her through the streets to the cathedral, where she was brutally murdered and her bones burned. Her death marks the end of the great age of Greek mathematics.

Orestes was deeply grieved over Hypatia's death. He felt responsible and determined to seek justice. When he went to Rome to ask the authorities to investigate her murder, they were indifferent.

"Hypatia is currently living in Athens," the official report read. "There has been no tragedy. The case is closed."

Although Hypatia made many important contributions to mathematics and science, few women have adopted her interests—until recently. Some historians believe that Hypatia's horrible death may have discouraged other women from becoming mathematicians. Still others believe that Hypatia's life— not her death— is the perfect symbol of what women or men can achieve when they work hard and stand up for what they believe is right.

JOHN NAPIER (*NAY-peer*), 1550–1617, was a Scottish nobleman who loved mathematics. He invented logarithms, worked in spherical trigonometry, and designed "Napier's rods," a mechanical calculating aid.

Magician or Mathematician?

"**E**xcuse me, friend, but isn't that Merchiston Castle up there on the hill?" the traveler asked with a hopeful gleam in his eye.

"That it is!" responded the old farmer as he patted his tired horse.

"I thought so!"

"Are you friends of the baron's family, then?" asked the farmer.

"Oh, no. We've never met," said the traveler. "I hail from Dundee. But I've heard terrible stories of his magic and black arts. I said to the wife, 'Next time I'm in Edinburgh, I'm going to get a look at the place for myself.' "

"Well, you look all you want, but you won't see any magic," the farmer replied. "The baron is just a smart man with a lot of ideas and energy. He doesn't need to use any magic."

"But how can you know that?" the visitor asked.

"I've been working for the Merchiston estate since the baron was a wee little one," said the farmer. "This is his field right here, and you know what? Because of his experiments with farming, we've got the best crop of oats we've ever had. I can't tell you exactly what we're using on this field, but it's working. No sir, there's no magic—there's just brains."

"But what about that story about the rooster?" the visitor asked. "Were you around here when that happened?"

"You can bet I was. I never saw such foolishness, but the baron is always willing to help fools fulfill themselves," laughed the farmer. "You see, he had hired a new batch of workers several months earlier. Then he began to suspect that at least one of them was stealing. At first there wasn't much missing—just a little feed and a tool here and there. But when the cook noticed some of her favorite kitchen things disappearing, well, the baron decided to take action."

The horse jingled its reins and shook its head, reminding the farmer that evening was approaching.

"I'd better get back to work. I've got to finish this field before sundown."

"But you've got to finish this story first," pleaded the traveler.

"All right, but it will have to be quick. Here's what happened. I think you'll agree that I have a smart master. He took his black rooster—the one without a speck of white anywhere—and put him into a dark storage room in the barn. Then he sent the workers in one at a time with instructions to pat the rooster on the back. You see, he'd told them earlier that this rooster could tell if people were honest or not—and since none of them would admit to stealing, he was forced to let the rooster do the telling.

"One by one the workers went in and patted the rooster on the back. The baron had told them that was necessary for the rooster to tell the truth. Then each person came back out and waited for the others. When they were all outside, the baron asked each worker to hold out his hands, palms up. All of them had black stains on their palms, except one. He was the thief, all right!"

"But I don't understand," said the visitor. "I thought you said he didn't use magic, and now you tell me about this magical rooster that can tell if someone's lying or not."

"If you'll be quiet, I'll finish the story," the farmer said. "You see, the workers didn't know that the baron had rubbed that rooster all full of lampblack, collected when we cleaned the oil lamps. The workers who had nothing to hide went right up and patted that rooster. But the one who felt guilty wasn't about to take a chance, so he didn't touch it. That's why his hands were clean."

The traveler sputtered, "Well, I'll be—."

"Nice chattin' with you, but I've got to get on with the field," the farmer said. "Got chores to do, too."

"Wait!" the traveler called after him. "Do you know the story about the pigeons? Now, that one's hard to explain!"

In Merchiston Castle, it was almost dinner time. John Napier, the eighth Laird of Merchiston, sat busily writing at his desk. Much of the day had been taken up with petty problems managing the estate. Finally he was able to give a few moments to his favorite hobby—mathematics.

He was polishing up an invention. Napier hoped this invention would help mathematicians, and especially astronomers, do their difficult computations more easily. This had not been a quick project; it had taken nearly twenty years to complete. Finally, Napier felt it was ready to be tested.

Napier had invented *logarithms*. This was a new method that made numerical calculations easier, more accurate, and less time-consuming. His method reduced multiplying and dividing to adding and subtracting. It saved an enormous amount of time—especially when working with large numbers.

Word spread quickly throughout Europe, and everyone who worked with numbers praised the marvelous discovery. Astronomers were especially pleased. They measured very large distances—like the distance between stars—so they had to work with very big numbers. Pierre Laplace, who lived two hundred years after Napier, said that logarithms, "by shortening the labors, doubled the life of the astronomer."

Napier was not the first person in his family to achieve fame. In fact, portraits of famous soldiers and statesmen lined the hallways of Merchiston Castle. His uncle, Adam Bothwell, had assisted at the marriage of Queen Mary and later crowned the infant King James VI.

Perhaps the legacy of a famous military family inspired Napier to dream up a collection of weapons for the future. He predicted the invention of sailing devices that would travel underwater. He imagined moving vehicles that could shoot in all directions as they moved. He also described a gun that could kill all cattle within a mile's radius. Some of these ideas were even too horrible for Napier to dwell on—later he refused to discuss them with his friends. But in World War II, his visions became reality with the use of the submarine, the military tank, and the machine gun.

Napier did not have a profession or an official government position. However, he was always involved in political and religious issues. He wrote many essays and arguments defending his ideas. At the University of St. Andrews, where he studied philosophy and theology, he was known for his quick temper. But he learned that when he became tense or discouraged, he could always turn to mathematics or astronomy to relax.

Some of Napier's contemporaries were famous for their long, involved computations. The trigonometry that Rheticus published in 1596 showed pages and pages of difficult calculations. Vieta, the famous French thinker, spent days just doing arithmetic. Napier suspected that sometimes mathematicians actually enjoyed making their work look complicated. He preferred the easy way.

In an effort to make arithmetic easier for bookkeepers and accountants, as well as for scholars and astronomers, Napier invented his famous rods. These were an assortment of rods marked off with numbers. When these rods were arranged correctly, they could be used for multiplication and division, and for taking square roots of numbers. They were a sort of movable multiplication table—an early type of slide rule, which is what people used before pocket calculators. Because they were often made of bone or ivory strips they were sometimes called "Napier's Bones." Today, Napier's rods are usually made of cardboard strips. They may seem clumsy compared to a pocket calculator, but in Napier's day they were a great help to people who worked with numbers.

Napier's desire to simplify computations led him to try other ideas. Once he designed a kind of "chess arithmetic" in which numbers were moved around like rooks and bishops on a chess board. That idea didn't work out, but another idea did take hold. He introduced the use of the decimal point to separate the whole number part from the fraction part of a number. This quickly became standard practice in Great Britain.

Magician or Mathematician?

Most of the common folk who lived around Merchiston Castle near Edinburgh had no understanding of what Napier was doing. For that matter, neither did his upper-class associates—he once complained that they couldn't do much more than "count on the fingers of their mail-clad hands." Although Napier's accomplishments had nothing to do with the supernatural, it was easier for people to explain them away as "magic." They didn't recognize his hard work and careful scientific processes. After all, there was that story about the pigeons.

"Hey, chap! Aren't you the man who told me the story about Napier and the rooster a couple weeks ago?" It was the traveler from Dundee, pausing at the roadside to wipe his brow. "I've been hoping to run into you so I could ask you again about that pigeon story."

The tired farmer groaned. He was about to steal a moment of rest at his favorite spot near the shore. Might as well give the fellow what he wants, he thought.

"All right, it goes like this. The baron's neighbor was raising pigeons some years ago, but he couldn't seem to keep them at home. Those hungry birds kept coming over to our fields and eating the grain out of the ground before it could even sprout. We warned the neighbor, but it didn't do any good. Finally, the baron had enough. He sent a personal message saying he was going to catch those birds and put them in a cage the next time they flew over his fields.

"The neighbor sent back the message 'You can have them if you can catch them,' knowing full well that no one could catch a flock of pigeons.

"But the next morning, when we came to begin work, we saw the baron himself out in the yard, scooping those pigeons up into a sack."

The traveler stood with his mouth open, ready for the explanation. The old farmer rubbed his beard, covering a trace of a smile. Shall I tell him about how the baron fed the pigeons peas soaked in brandy? he wondered to himself.

Impatient, the traveler demanded, "Well, go on. How did he do it?"

"I dunno. Just magic, I guess."

GALILEO GALILEI (*gal-i-LAY-o gal-i-LAY-ee*), 1564–1642, was an Italian astronomer who made a notable contribution to mathematics. He helped introduce the scientific method, which emphasizes the importance of both experiment and theory.

Seeing Isn't Believing

"Enrico, how would you like to help me tomorrow with an important experiment?" asked the professor.

"You know I'm always ready to help you, Professor Galilei. What do you have in mind?"

"Do you remember in class when we were discussing Aristotle's theory of falling objects?"

"Yes, of course," the student answered.

"Enrico, I am now prepared to demonstrate to my students and my colleagues here at Pisa that Aristotle was wrong."

The young student tried to swallow his surprise. He said, "That will be no easy task. All the other professors here are sure that Aristotle was correct. How can you possibly change their minds?"

"Meet me tomorrow morning at the Tower of Pisa," Galileo replied. "The fact that it leans will be perfect for our needs. See if you can get Roberto to come and help us. I am posting notices on the doors—I hope a big crowd will come and watch. Truth will finally have its day!"

The next day the professor and his two students met at the base of the leaning tower. Galileo was exuberant, practically breathless at the thought of what he was about to do. Quickly, he explained the plan to Enrico and Roberto.

"You see that I have two iron balls. One of them is light, but the other weighs ten times as much. According to Aristotle, the speed of an object's fall is proportional to its weight—heavier objects fall faster. So everyone will expect that the larger ball will fall ten times as fast as the smaller one." The two students nodded. Galileo continued excitedly, "I'm going to climb to the top of the tower. You stay here and watch. When you see me wave from the balcony, adjust your timepieces. You must be prepared to show the crowd how long it took for each of the balls to hit the ground. Enrico, you time the small one. Roberto, watch the larger. Any questions?"

"You know we respect you, sir, but what if—" Enrico broke off in the middle of his sentence. He wanted to ask his professor what he would do if the experiment failed—but as he looked at Galileo's excited face, he lost his courage.

Students and teachers were gathering around the tower courtyard. The students joked and laughed with each other, glad for a break from their studies. The professors also joked, but more quietly. They were embarrassed for Galileo.

"I can't believe Galileo is such a fool. Why must he flaunt his ignorance before the whole city?"

Another asked, "Do you think he will ever grow up? He is twenty-five years old already, much too old for this nonsense."

"Aristotle must be turning over in his grave," said a third. "Imagine the arrogance of questioning Aristotle!"

Finally, just before the stroke of noon, Galileo was ready. Enrico and Roberto craned their necks to see him at the top of the tower.

The crowd became quiet. Then Galileo signalled his young assistants and dropped both of the iron balls at the same instant.

In just a few moments both balls hit the ground. Enrico and Roberto believed and trusted Galileo, but they were as surprised as everyone else. The two weights landed at exactly the same moment. The heavier one had *not* traveled ten times as fast as the lighter one. On this matter, Aristotle had made a mistake.

Galileo was joyful as he scurried down the tower stairs. But his joy diminished when he reached the courtyard. Only a few students remained to congratulate him. His colleagues had gone back to their work, muttering on their way about magic and illusion. Even though they had seen the experiment with their own eyes, they refused to believe what they had seen. Galileo was in trouble.

It wasn't the first time. Years earlier, Galileo's father, Vincenzio, had scolded his son and warned him that he would turn out worthless. The boy didn't seem interested in working hard or making money. The problem was not lack of talent. In fact, Galileo was clearly a gifted child. He was especially good in music and art, and his father hoped that he would use these talents to make money. But Vincenzio knew it was difficult to get rich by singing or painting. He himself was an accomplished musician, but he had to support the family by selling cloth.

Eventually his family decided that Galileo should become a doctor. He was sent to the University of Pisa to study medicine. But Galileo wasn't interested. The lectures were boring, the professors' ideas were old-fashioned, and the students were never allowed to experiment on patients or cadavers.

One day as young Galileo walked through the halls, he noticed a classroom door propped open. Inside, the students sat up in their seats, alert and interested. They were obviously fascinated by the subject being discussed—geometry. Galileo loitered outside the door, eavesdropping. It was a new subject for the young medical student, and he found it very exciting. Soon he began skipping his medical classes to attend mathematics lectures.

Galileo didn't know what to do. He knew he was supposed to follow his father's plan for him, but his heart just wasn't in it. One day he went to the university cathedral to pray, hoping for an answer that would give him peace. But what happened in the cathedral stirred him up so much that he didn't sleep for days.

It was late afternoon when Galileo entered the cathedral. While he prayed and meditated, a worker came in to light the lamps. Huge brass lamps hung on chains from the ceiling. To light them, a worker stood on a balcony and hooked each chain with a long pole. He pulled the chain and the lamp hanging from it towards his flame. When each lamp was lit, he released it and it swung back and forth like a pendulum until it finally came to rest.

Galileo had seen this process before, but this time he noticed something new. He observed that whether it swung in a wide or narrow arc, each swing of the lamp took the same time. To make sure he wasn't just imagining this, he checked the time of the swings with his own heart's pulse.

Back in his room, Galileo began experimenting with all sorts of hanging objects. He borrowed chains and scraps of iron from a nearby metal worker. He discovered that neither the size of the arc nor the weight of the hanging object affected the time of the swing. Only the length of the chain did that. Galileo had discovered the law of the pendulum. At first Galileo was interested in using his discovery to disprove Aristotle's theories on falling objects. If Aristotle were correct, a heavy weight on a swinging chain would swing to the bottom faster than a light weight—but the two weights reached the bottom at the same time. This is when he got the idea of climbing the Tower of Pisa. However, he did make a practical invention based on his findings. This was the pulse counter, widely used by doctors to check their patients' heart rates. Eventually, Galileo's discovery about swinging objects led to the invention of the pendulum clock.

All these late-night experiments didn't help Galileo's grades. Before long his father paid a visit to see what was going on.

"What's wrong with you, my son?" he scowled. "Don't you know mathematicians can't make a living? We need your help at home. If you can't get a decent job as a doctor and send us money, you may as well come home and work in the store."

Galileo thought about his parents and his six younger brothers and sisters. Part of him felt guilty for not doing what his father wanted—yet he couldn't tolerate studying subjects that didn't interest him.

"I'm sorry, father. I will try to make you proud of me. Remember how I used to make toys for us children? Perhaps I can invent some little things to sell. I will send you money as soon as I can, but please don't make me give up studying mathematics."

Exasperated, his father Vincenzio waved goodbye and left Galileo to his own foolishness, as he considered it. Galileo never overcame his sense of family responsibility. Often he went without things he needed so he could send his younger brothers and sisters money.

Perhaps if Vincenzio had seen the other professors hiss Galileo at the Tower of Pisa that day in 1590, he would have regretted allowing his son to give up medicine. His colleagues' scorn disturbed Galileo, but he was never sorry he had chosen mathematics. Soon he left Pisa for the University of Padua, where he taught for 18 years.

At Padua, the university was more open-minded, and Galileo was allowed to continue his controversial experiments and writing. One day he heard some amazing news. A Dutch spectacle maker named Hans Lippershey had accidentally discovered that combining glass lenses in a certain way made objects viewed through them appear up to three times larger than life. Lippershey and his apprentice had sold several of these telescopes as toys. Galileo set to work and made his own telescopes, but his were definitely not toys. Rather, they opened the skies for human study.

Every night Galileo looked heavenward. He was amazed to see craters on the moon. He tracked the path of Venus and noted the rings of Saturn. Most importantly, he discovered in 1610 that Jupiter had satellites or moons in orbit around it. This observation confirmed what the astronomer Copernicus had taught—that smaller bodies revolve around larger ones. This had led Copernicus to claim that the earth was not the center of the universe, as everyone believed, but one of many planets orbiting the sun.

Galileo was in trouble again. The authorities and the church believed that Copernicus was a radical, opposed to everything they taught. In fact, they made it illegal to read, study, or teach Copernicus's ideas. Galileo tried to obey that law, but he found it very difficult.

Hundreds of people came to look through Galileo's telescopes. Most of them found it entertaining and amusing; few recognized the telescope's scientific importance. Military authorities welcomed Galileo's invention; now they could see the enemy approaching at sea before the enemy could see them. But seeing *wasn't* believing: like the professors at the leaning tower, many people refused to accept the truth. Some even refused to look through the glass. They didn't want to change their familiar ideas and admit that Galileo might be right about the universe.

During the last eight years of his life, the church authorities watched Galileo very closely. He was not free to speak or write about his beliefs or observations. The authorities threatened to torture him if he would not recant—take back—his scientific findings. Finally he gave in—so instead of being tortured, he was sentenced to live in seclusion the rest of his life.

In 1638 Galileo became totally blind.

"Professor Galileo?"

"Yes. Who is it?"

"It's Roberto. Roberto Lozano. I don't suppose you remember me. I was your student at Pisa."

"At Pisa? Surely not the Roberto who helped with the experiment at the tower?"

"Yes, yes, professor. That's me."

"Oh my, my. What brings you here now? I'm not doing crazy experiments anymore."

"But they weren't crazy," Roberto cried. "That's why I've come. I wanted to thank you for inspiring me. I believe in you and in what you stand for. I always have, and always will."

"Thank you, son. I hope there will be others to carry on the search for truth. I can't do much now that I'm blind, even if I were allowed to work."

"Your eyes may be blind, professor, but you are the only one who has really seen the truth," said Roberto. "Someday the world will realize that you were right. Someday they'll be sorry they treated you this way."

"Well, maybe so." The old professor shook his head in doubt. He'd have to see it to believe it.

BLAISE PASCAL (*blez pahs-KAHL*), 1623–1662, was a French thinker, mathematician, and scientist. He made many invaluable contributions to mathematics and physics, and is also remembered for his religious and philosophical writings.

Count on Pascal

"I just don't know what to do with young Blaise," Etienne Pascal complained to a clerk at his law office.

"What's the matter? Won't he do his studies?"

"It's just the opposite, I'm afraid," Pascal explained. "He won't quit. Especially when it comes to mathematics. He needs to concentrate more on his languages. I even tried locking up all my physics and mathematics books, but the boy hounds me day and night to answer his questions."

"That is an odd problem," laughed the clerk. "I wish my Hugo shared it. But I'm sorry to laugh. You seem seriously concerned."

"Yes, I am," nodded Pascal. "Last week one day—promise you won't tell anyone?"

"I promise. Go ahead."

"Well, last week one day when I got home from the office, I found Blaise on the floor, drawing and figuring. He has never seen a book on geometry, you understand. He's only twelve years old, remember? And I have not taught him even what I know. But there he was, and in front of him was the proof that the sum of the angles of any triangle equals two right angles. I tell you, friend, it made me quiver to see it."

"Etienne, I think you should quit fighting it. Admit that your son has special talent, and help him develop. Who knows, he might discover something useful someday!"

So Etienne Pascal quit fighting his son. He unlocked the books, and unlocked a world of new excitement for Blaise.

As a young man, Blaise sometimes wondered what it would have been like to have a mother. His had died when he was only four years old. But his two sisters, Gilberte and Jacqueline, were deeply devoted to him, and his father—well, his father did everything he could to make sure the family was comfortable, happy, and well-educated.

Blaise and his sisters might have enjoyed going to school, but their father kept them home and taught them himself. He thought this would be best because Blaise was often sick. In fact, when he was a baby, the doctors said he would probably not live long. Like most parents, the Pascals were willing to try anything to save their little son. When he was one year old, Blaise was "cured" by a folk doctor using a special poultice—a warm mixture made using a special recipe. Legend said that nine leaves of three special herbs should be used, and the herbs had to be gathered by a seven-year-old child before sunrise. Whether this home remedy saved him is questionable, but there is no question about the remarkable impact this little boy's life would have on mathematics.

One day Etienne interrupted Blaise's reading with an exciting proposal.

"How would you like to go with me this afternoon to the Free

Academy? Some fascinating ideas are being discussed there and I'd like to take you along."

"Oh, thank you, Father! I'd love to go."

Blaise knew that many of Paris's most distinguished scientists and mathematicians gathered regularly at the academy to discuss their studies and experiments.

The fourteen-year-old listened quietly, spellbound by the wonderful ideas and powerful words of some of the most brilliant men alive. He began to attend regularly and soon entered into the discussions, surprising the older men with how much he understood.

In 1640 his father was appointed administrator of taxes in the city of Rouen. It was an important position with heavy responsibilities. Blaise adjusted to the move to Rouen easily, quickly making friends with other persons studying mathematics.

When Blaise was nineteen, one ordinary night turned into a momentous occasion. The streets of Rouen were quiet, and the night was comfortably cool, but Blaise couldn't sleep. His legs felt stiff and his head ached just enough to keep him awake. Hard as he tried, he couldn't help hearing his father's sighs from the next room. Exhausted after poring over his books all evening, Etienne Pascal groaned when the numbers refused to balance.

Blaise snuggled into the bed and covered his head with the comforter. But it was no use. In his imagination, he saw the fatigue and frustration on his father's face. He began to regret that his father had taken the prestigious job. Perhaps they should have stayed in Paris, after all.

Finally, attempting to talk himself out of his sleeplessness, Blaise made a promise.

"I will help Father somehow with his work. There must be an easier way to balance his figures!"

The next morning, a haggard Blaise crawled out of bed and began work on what was to be the first calculating machine. It was not an instant invention: its requirements were fairly complex. But Blaise was determined to make his father's accounting easier.

After many tries, Blaise finally got all the gears of his "arithmetic machine" to work. It was later recognized as the first calculator. One of the original models was presented to the king, and a duplicate was given to the royal chancellor. And of course Blaise gave one to his father to make his accounting easier. Most of Blaise's friends considered the calculating machine to be his greatest contribution to mathematics. Perhaps that is why he is regarded today as the "father of the computer age,"—and why one of our most valuable computer languages is named "Pascal."

Jacqueline loved her brother Blaise dearly, and she understood his commitment to study, but sometimes she wished he would take a rest.

"Blaise, it's time for dinner," she called for the third time.
When there was no response, she went into the study to see what was going on.

"Jacqueline," Blaise grinned in surprise, "I'm glad you've come. I have something truly remarkable to show you!"
Jacqueline went to the desk and looked over his shoulder. She saw numbers arranged in the shape of a triangle. "What's so remarkable about this?" she demanded.

"Look, Jacqueline. This number array has been around for centuries, but I'm discovering some new patterns in it. Each time I find one, it leads me to find more. I'm not sure there's an end to the number of patterns in this arrangement."

He took a pen from the desk and pointed to the horizontal rows. "For instance, all of these rows add up to powers of two. And if you move diagonally, like this, the sums of any column can be found here."

Blaise excitedly moved his pointer around the triangle, showing Jacqueline pattern after pattern that he had found. Soon both of their dinners were cold. During his continued studies, Pascal found so many patterns in the triangle of numbers that it was given his name—Pascal's Triangle.

```
            1
          1   1
        1   2   1
      1   3   3   1
    1   4   6   4   1
  1   5  10  10   5   1
1   6  15  20  15   6   1
```

The Pascal family wa s fascinated by mathematics and science, but they were also interested in philosophy and religion. After miraculously escaping death in an accident, Blaise quit studying mathematics and science. Instead, he gave his attention to questions about ethics and morality—the study of right and wrong. He was convinced that these areas of study were most important, and that he should not think about mathematics again.

One night when Blaise was suffering from insomnia, he began to feel a terrible toothache. Soon the pain throbbed in his jaw; his whole head felt ready to explode. In most parts of Europe at that time, the closest thing to a dentist was a barber with a pair of pliers. The thought of someone coming at his mouth was enough to keep Blaise awake until morning.

Finally, in desperation, Blaise tried to distract himself from the pain. He began to think about the *cycloid*—the curve traced by a point on a circle as the circle rolls along a straight line. Many of the mathematicians of the time were baffled by questions about this geometric shape. Ideas filled his mind and suddenly he noticed that his toothache was gone!

Blaise took the disappearing toothache as a sign that it was permissible to study mathematics again. For eight days he worked enthusiastically on the cycloid, developing a complete set of ideas about the curve. He proved that the fastest path between any two non-vertical points is *not* a straight line, but the cycloid. He also discovered that two or more steel balls, released from different points on a cycloid track at the same time, would reach the end of the track at the same moment. His contemporaries, who had been trying to solve these problems for years, were astonished.

"My dear Monsieur Pascal," began a letter that Blaise received in 1654, "I would like your help with a practical problem. You see, I am a professional gambler, and my outstanding reputation is about to be ruined! I am enclosing a copy of the arithmetic I used to figure out my chances of winning at dice. The numbers say I should be winning, but I am losing money every day. Please hurry with an answer!"

Now Blaise was not particularly interested in helping gamblers, but the mathematics of the problem hooked him. Not only did he see the famous gambler's mathematical error, but he began to think of other possibilities: how could mathematics predict chance or luck?

He wrote to Pierre de Fermat, considered to be the leading mathematician of the day. Their work on this problem formed the basis of probability theory, the branch of mathematics that predicts the chance that something will occur.

During his relatively short lifetime, Blaise Pascal made many significant discoveries. Some of them, like the calculator, were practical. He is also credited with inventing the first one-wheeled wheelbarrow. He even designed a bus and made other suggestions for Paris's public transportation system. Other discoveries were stepping stones for later mathematicians. His research on atmospheric pressure and the vacuum established principles crucial to the study of physics. His work on "Pascal's Triangle" invites more analysis and discovery.

Pascal was not interested in becoming wealthy or famous. Rather, he tried to practice generosity and compassion for others. In June 1662 he invited a poor homeless family to live in his home. When several members of the family became ill with smallpox, he moved in with his sister Gilberte rather than force the poor family to move. Two months later, after suffering from intense pain, he died of cancer at the age of thirty-nine.

Several weeks later, Gilberte and her housekeeper went to her brother's home to sort through his possessions. Deciding what was valuable and what should be discarded was no easy task. Then Gilberte discovered something odd.

"Suzanne, come look at this," she urged.

Suzanne crossed the room to Blaise's desk. Gilberte had opened several drawers. Each was filled with bits and scraps of paper, some torn, some folded.

"It looks like each piece of paper has a separate idea on it—as if

Blaise had recorded his thoughts whenever and wherever they came to him," Gilberte said to herself.

"Shall I get a waste can, ma'am?" the housekeeper asked. "Perhaps it would be easiest to just dump the whole drawer at once."

Gilberte didn't answer. She was absorbed in reading the fragments. Suzanne went to a closet and began pulling out boxes. When she opened one, her gasp caught Gilberte's attention.

"What is it, Suzanne?"

"Three boxes filled with more of the same, ma'am!" she said. "It's too bad we'll never know what they were—"

"Wait!" interrupted Gilberte. "In this box, the pieces are sewn together with string, as if he wanted to publish them in this order. I'd better take a closer look at this!"

After examining the fragments, Gilberte decided that Blaise's insights should be preserved, so she organized them into a book called *Pensées*, "thoughts." This rich storehouse of ideas has been an important influence on theologians and philosophers since Pascal's day. *Pensées* includes hundreds of short sayings such as "When we read too fast or too slowly, we understand nothing," and "Do you wish people to believe good of you? Don't speak." The sayings reflect Pascal's careful reasoning and his sincere attempt to understand life.

In one entry, Pascal writes:

> When I consider the short duration of my life, swallowed up in
> the eternity before and after, the little space that I fill and even
> can see . . . I am frightened and astonished at being here rather
> than there; for there is no reason why here rather than there,
> why now rather than then.

Pascal could not have realized what a *big* space he filled in the history of mathematics, nor how his short life would make such an impression on thoughtful people everywhere.

SIR ISAAC NEWTON, 1642–1727, an Englishman, is recognized around the world as one of the greatest figures in the history of mathematics and science. He explained the laws of motion and gravitation, made important discoveries about light and color, and developed calculus.

The Short Giant

The exhausted farmer wiped his hands on his pants and headed for the house. The milking was finished at last. "This breeze could blow up a shower," he thought. "Maybe I'll get some rest tomorrow."

He looked up at the trees silhouetted against the moonlit sky, their branches bending in the soft wind. Night had just fallen on the Lincolnshire countryside. Suddenly he stopped in his tracks, rubbed his eyes, and squinted at the sky beyond the tree. Was that a light? It couldn't be. Yet even as he watched, the glow grew larger and then fainter; it seemed to float over his field of oats.

Hurrying to the house, he opened the door and shouted, "Emmaline, come here quickly! I want you to see something!"

His wife set down the loaf of bread she had just taken from the oven and went to the door. "What is it, Henry?"

"Look—over there—see that light? What do you suppose it is?"

She clutched his arm and stared in disbelief. "It must be the comet Mrs. Martin was talking about today at the market. She said she and Mr. Martin saw it last night, but you know how she is. None of us really believed her. Now I'm so ashamed. Do you think it means any harm, Henry?"

Henry didn't know what to think, but he lay awake a long time that night trying to figure it out. On Saturday, when the village farmers gathered in town for their weekly visit, all they could talk about were the strange lights. Everyone had a theory about them, but no one knew anything for sure. The townsfolk described their sightings to each other in detail, and a frightened hush hung over the group.

On the fringes stood Mr. Clark, the village pharmacist. He listened quietly for a while, smiling to himself, but finally he could restrain himself no longer. "My friends," he began, "you have nothing to fear. Do you know young Isaac Newton, the boy who is living with us while he attends King's School? He's a very clever lad, and I'm sure he meant no harm. The comets you have been seeing—" he broke into a broad grin—"are merely kites made by the boy and fitted with lanterns."

At first the embarrassed farmers were resentful. They were angry that a mere boy could make them look so foolish. But eventually, as they heard more and more about Isaac Newton's "contraptions," they overcame their anger. They grew to respect his ability to design inventions like none they had ever seen. Most of these inventions were not very practical. In fact, they were more like toys. Isaac made a wooden model of a windmill, which really pumped water. Then he made a clock that ran and kept time using water power. He made a mechanical carriage that a child could drive. And he made a miniature mill to grind wheat, complete with a live mouse harnessed to turn the wheel.

The Clarks were fascinated by Isaac's skills. He was a courteous boy and they enjoyed having him live with them—but they were concerned that his creativity was channeled into play rather than schoolwork. They felt a little responsible; after all, Isaac's mother and stepfather had sent him to live with the Clarks specifically so he could go to school. He was clearly not meant to follow in his father's footsteps as a farmer. Although he had good intentions, he always got involved in reading, and forgot to watch the sheep or come home in time to milk. No, he had to get an education, but school wasn't exactly his favorite pastime.

Studying Latin and the classics might be fine for some boys, but Isaac wasn't interested in those subjects. He'd much rather have class in Mr. Clark's attic, surrounded by the apothecary's books about chemicals. The colored bottles and shelves of apparatus kept Isaac's imagination so busy that he could have spent weeks there.

"Master Isaac, how does it feel to be the class dunce?" the village bully taunted one day on the way to school. It wasn't the first time. Usually Isaac just ignored him and continued to think about what he would do after school.

"I'm third out of twenty," the bully jeered, trying to make Isaac react. "Don't ignore me, you puny little runt. I'll teach you a thing or two." With that, he swung his leg up and kicked his heavy boot into Isaac's stomach.

Isaac had had enough. He challenged his antagonist to fight that day after school. They met on a field near the schoolyard, surrounded by a crowd of schoolmates who had heard about the match during the day. Everyone knew that Isaac would be beaten; they just didn't know how badly.

When it was time to fight, Isaac clenched his teeth and his fists, harnessing all his built-up frustration and anger. His first punch missed, but then his punches met their target—squarely in the jaw. The stunned bully was no match for Isaac's fury. In just a few minutes, Isaac had given him a black eye and several other bruises. Isaac was clearly winning when the schoolmaster hurried over and stopped the fight. Even he must have been impressed by the power hidden in the small, quiet student. Instead of scolding Isaac, he offered him this challenge: "You've beaten your foe on the field—now let's see if you can beat him in the classroom as well."

Isaac accepted the challenge. He began to study and concentrate on his schoolwork. He made phenomenal progress. By the end of the year he had not only passed the bully, but was at the head of the class.

When Isaac's stepfather died and his mother needed help on the farm, Isaac decided to go home. He determined to be a successful farmer. Before long, however, his old habits reappeared as Isaac immersed himself in reading and "tinkering." His mother agreed with his teachers and the local minister: Isaac must be sent to Cambridge for university studies.

At Trinity College in Cambridge, Isaac was not a remarkable student. His work was average. He was quiet, usually alone. One day at the Stourbridge Fair, Isaac bought a used book on astronomy. He became fascinated with the planets and the sun and moon, but as he read he realized there was much in this book that he could not understand. He would need to study geometry and trigonometry first. That was the beginning of his interest in mathematics. Isaac began to read and learn from the great masters. Euclid, Descartes, and Kepler became his teachers.

"Excuse me, young man. You're Master Isaac Newton, aren't you?" The robed professor grinned down at Isaac, sitting under a tree reading. "I have been looking forward to meeting you. I am Isaac Barrow, professor of mathematics."

Meeting Isaac Barrow was one of the luckiest events of Isaac Newton's life. Professor Barrow was not only an outstanding teacher; he was also a dynamic personality who challenged and encouraged his students to achieve their best. The two Isaacs became good friends who worked together with mutual respect.

Isaac Newton had just begun some exciting projects when London was hit by an outbreak of plague. Bubonic plague was a deadly, highly contagious disease that could kill thousands of people in days. Because Cambridge wasn't far from London, the university was closed and the students sent home. Isaac went back to his mother's farm in Lincolnshire. For a year and a half he waited for the school to reopen, but the plague was not easily stamped out. Thousands of people died. Then, in 1666, London suffered another heavy blow when a great fire burned half the city. Although 13,200 homes and 90 churches were destroyed, the fire helped London in one way: the plague was finally extinguished.

Back at Cambridge, Newton's professors were surprised to see how much he had accomplished without them. In fact, he started work on many of his great discoveries during that time alone on the farm.

Isaac Barrow recognized genius when he saw it. Before long he requested that Newton replace him as professor at the university. In this capacity, Newton would have the time and resources he needed to pursue his research. As a professor, he lectured once a week, usually for about an hour. Each week, students who wanted to discuss the previous week's lecture could come to his office with their questions. Most of his time was reserved for study, which suited Newton very well. He taught at Cambridge for eighteen years.

During his first years of teaching, Newton lectured on optics—the study of light and vision. He shared the fascinating results of his studies, showing how white light could be broken down into colors using a prism. He showed the telescopes he had built and explained how the giant lenses worked. His theories were published and read around the world. They also created controversy, which Newton hated. He vowed not to publish his ideas again. Defending them took too much of his valuable time, he said. Thus, many of his great discoveries lay buried in his desk for years.

Eventually, Newton's work was displayed for all to see. In addition to his work on light, he made discoveries in astronomy and mathematics. He was the first to scientifically establish the theory of universal gravitation. This theory showed that the same force that makes an apple fall to the ground holds the moon and the planets in place—gravity. These discoveries about motion greatly influenced science.

In mathematics, Newton demonstrated an amazing ability to solve problems. Although he worked in many branches of mathematics, he is best known for developing the binomial theorem and calculus.

Newton was not interested in ideas for their own sake. He wanted to make discoveries that would help people understand the physical world and the universe. His mathematical findings did just that. They gave mathematicians and scientists the tools to solve problems that previously had been unsolvable.

When Newton's three-volume book *Principia* (Principles) was published, scholars around the world quickly recognized Newton's brilliant achievement. The famous German mathematician Leibniz said, "Taking mathematics from the beginning of the world to the time when Newton lived, what he did was much the better half." Alexander Pope wrote these lines:

> Nature and Nature's laws lay hid in night;
> God said, "Let Newton be," and all was light.

In spite of all the praise he received, Isaac Newton remained modest. He resisted publishing his ideas, and always had to be persuaded by colleagues to release his latest work.

Often he was asked how he did it—what was his secret of discovery. Newton insisted that he was no different from the average person, except in perseverance and vigilance. "When I am working on something," he said, "I am always thinking about it. This takes much patience. I keep the subject of my inquiry constantly before me, and wait."

Newton's powers of concentration were so strong that he was often accused of being absentminded. His friends complained that he forgot to eat and sleep. Once when Newton had guests for dinner, he excused himself to get more wine—but he never returned to the table. His guests later found him with the unopened bottle of wine in his study; on the way back to the table he had stopped to write down an idea and completely forgotten his visitors. Another time, according to legend, he was leading his horse uphill. The horse got away, but Newton didn't realize she was gone until he got to the top of the hill and tried to jump into the saddle.

In his later years, Newton got involved in politics. He served one term in Parliament and directed the mint, where money is coined. He was appointed president of the Royal Society, where England's leading mathematicians and philosophers exchanged ideas. Although he turned his attention to other concerns, he never lost his remarkable power to solve problems. His approach was the scientific method: experiment, analyze, and experiment some more.

Isaac Newton's appearance was undistinguished. He was born prematurely and wasn't expected to live. Short and puny, he was shy and often melancholy. Until he reached college, he was a poor student, considered lazy by his teachers. But he came to be almost universally ranked as the greatest mathematician who ever lived. During his lifetime, Newton was quick to acknowledge that no mathematician works alone. He recognized and encouraged others in their studies, and he knew that he owed a debt to the past. He said, "If I have seen farther than others, it is because I have stood on the shoulders of giants."

Since that day, every mathematician and scientist has stood on the shoulders of a giant—Isaac Newton.

LEONHARD EULER (*LAY-on-ard OY-ler*), 1707–1783, was an energetic and productive Swiss mathematician. In spite of blindness, he made important contributions to numerical analysis, calculus, and topology, a branch of geometry. Much of the mathematical notation used today stems from Euler.

The Blind Man Who Could See

It had been a calm day until their voices were heard on the street, boasting and scolding loudly as they approached.

"Look, I'm always very careful in my computations. You must have made a mistake."

"Me? Why don't you admit the truth for once? I've been studying longer than you have—I'm the senior student."

"Age and experience are no substitute for brains, my friend!"

The two young men hurried down the narrow cobblestone street, stopped abruptly in front of a door, and knocked. They paused to get their breath.

"Professor Euler, please," they said to the housekeeper, who ushered them into the professor's study. In their teacher's presence they were more subdued, but still tense.

"Professor Euler," one began. "We're sorry to bother you but Fritz and I can't seem to agree on the solution to that problem you gave us last week."

"What Nicholas means, sir, is that *he* can't seem to get the right answer."

Leonhard Euler smiled, perhaps remembering his own youthful vigor and competitive spirit. Although he was blind now, he could imagine the fierce enthusiasm in his students' eyes.

"What problem is troubling you?" he asked.

"It's the one where you asked us to add the first 17 terms in a convergent series of numbers," explained Nicholas. "I've finished it with no trouble, though I must admit it was a tedious, time-consuming task. I'm sure—"

"Finished isn't enough!" interrupted Fritz. "You've got to get it right."

"It's in the 50th decimal place that we disagree, Professor," Nicholas continued. "You can understand that I'm not eager to do that work all over again, especially when I'm sure my sum is correct."

And then, while they were still arguing, Professor Euler demonstrated his marvelous powers of concentration. Right there, standing in front of them—without any paper or pencil or calculator—Leonhard Euler did the problem in his head and announced the correct answer.

The two students were so amazed at his incredible mental powers that they forgot their argument. On their way home, they were still musing over the incident.

"Can you believe that anyone can add so many numbers in his mind?" Fritz didn't expect an answer. Both of the boys knew it was next to impossible—yet they had seen it with their very own eyes.

"Do you think it's easier for him because he's blind?" suggested Nicholas.

"Maybe. But I've heard stories about him doing these sorts of things even when he was our age, with two good eyes. Father told me that once when Professor Euler couldn't sleep, he multiplied each number from 1 to 100 by itself *six times*—in his head. Not only that, but several days later he could still remember the entire table!"

"It sounds crazy, but I believe you," said Nicholas. "We're pretty lucky to have him for a teacher. Some day, Fritz, he may be famous."

As a child, Leonhard Euler had been a cheerful, eager learner. He loved reading, music, and science. His father was the pastor of a small village church, and he hoped Leonhard would follow in his footsteps. But it was mathematics that came most naturally for Leonhard. Though he studied religion and accepted his father's beliefs, he chose to spend his life organizing mathematical thought and discovering new approaches to the mysterious world of numbers.

Sometimes Euler's friends feared that he loved mathematics too much. While he was teaching and researching at the St. Petersburg Academy in Russia, he was given an astronomy problem. He surprised many of Russia's finest scientists by constructing a complex solution in only three days. They had expected such work to take several months. But such concentration is not without cost. Within a few days, Euler got a high fever. The fever passed, but as a result of this illness, Euler lost the sight in his right eye.

Later, the mathematician developed a cataract in his left eye and began to lose his sight. Instead of despairing, he trained several of his sons and other assistants to take dictation. He had a large slate, or blackboard, brought in and mounted on a table. By the time he was completely blind, his helpers could write and edit whatever he told them. Whenever he had a concept that needed illustration, he would take the chalk and draw a few crude strokes on the slate that clarified his meaning. His assistants carefully copied the drawings for future use.

When Euler first accepted the fact that his blindness would be permanent, he told his friends, "Now I'll have fewer distractions." Apparently this was true, for the man who had already been producing scientific and mathematical papers at a phenomenal pace began producing even more.

Although Leonhard Euler was Swiss by birth, he spent most of his life working and teaching in Russia and Germany. He spoke German, French, and Russian, but usually wrote in Latin. Euler was the most productive writer mathematics has ever known. He wrote textbooks for Russian elementary schools. He wrote articles for other scholars. He wrote so much that upon his death it took 50 pages just to list the titles of his works. His output averaged 800 printed pages a year, not counting over 4,000 letters. He worked quickly, but carefully. Someone once asked him how he could write so quickly and still get everything right. "Oh," he replied, blushing, "my pencil is more intelligent than I am."

Most of Euler's writings were on mathematical topics, but he also applied mathematics to many practical areas. He wrote about guns, the northern lights, sound, navigation, shipbuilding, lotteries, magnetism, and astronomy, to name only a few subjects. One of his papers solved a famous problem that had confronted a German town earlier in the century.

It seems that the residents of Königsberg were planning a gala affair for their old city. They wanted to celebrate with a parade that would march past all the significant historical sites of the city. But the city was built on an island in the middle of the Pregel River, and connected to the surrounding land by seven bridges.

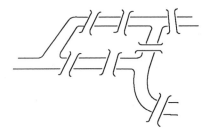

No one could plot a course for the parade that would cross each of the bridges once and only once. Euler was the first person to prove that the problem was impossible. The people of Königsberg had to give up seeking such a parade route. But as a result of this problem, Euler introduced a new area in mathematics called *topology*, a branch of geometry.

Everyone liked Euler. He was almost always cheerful and optimistic, and he especially loved children. He and Mrs. Euler had thirteen children, though only five lived to be adults. Euler would work on mathematics while bouncing a baby on one knee. He loved going with his children to puppet shows, and laughed so hard at the funny routines that the whole audience would laugh at *him*. Even with a room full of noisy children chasing cats, Euler could concentrate on his mathematics. If he was in the middle of a complicated problem when it was time for dinner, he took time out to eat and then continued afterward. This would not be so remarkable if his computations had been on paper or a calculator, but usually they were only in his head.

Many procedures and formulas used in mathematics today originated with Euler. Some even have his name attached. We use "Euler's line," "Euler's constant," and "Euler's angles."

"Euler's formula" is often used in geometry. He discovered that for certain solids, the number of faces plus the number of vertices equals the number of edges plus 2. Or,

$$F + V = E + 2$$

Euler also contributed to mathematics by establishing various symbols, or notation. He chose to use the Greek letter π (*pi*) for the ratio of the circumference to the diameter of a circle. This symbol had been used before, but Euler's use of it in textbooks made it widely known. He used the lower case letters *a*, *b*, and *c* for sides of a triangle, and the corresponding capitals *A*, *B*, and *C* for the opposite angles. And he simplified processes in algebra by introducing the notation *f(x)*. He influenced modern notation more than any other mathematician in history.

Euler's brilliant mind was a wonderful treasure; his unfaltering courage was probably just as valuable. Euler's most obvious problem was his blindness. While he didn't let it disrupt his work, surely it was discouraging not to be able to see his children and grandchildren, and not to be able to care for himself. Once, about five years after he became totally blind, the doctors operated in hopes of recovering his sight. The surgery was an amazing success, and for a short time Euler could see. But his eyes became infected, and after several days of intense pain, he was totally and permanently blind.

At about this time, Euler was working on a theory about the motion of the moon. The computations were incredibly long, and his assistants were busier than ever filling paper with Euler's dictation. The master would sketch curves and scribble formulas on his slate. They would record his findings, sometimes winking at each other as they noticed Euler's childlike enthusiasm.

One night, after a long day of work, the household was awakened by a clanging alarm. "Fire! Fire!" they cried. As he groped his way out of bed, Euler realized that the smell of smoke was already strong. He tried to shake off a sleepy feeling, but the confused cries of people in the street and the bells and loud noises made him feel like part of a horrible nightmare.

"Professor Euler! Are you all right?" It was Peter Grimm, his faithful Swiss servant. "We must hurry to escape! Here I am. Hold on to my neck now, and I'll carry you out on my back."

Grimm held on to Euler with one hand, and with the other shielded himself from the smoke, flames, and falling debris. Finally they were outside and safe with the others.

"Thank goodness you're safe, Professor Euler!" gasped his assistant. "I grabbed what I could of your papers about the moon. I'm not sure if I got everything, though."

"Don't worry about it son," Euler answered. "We can always do it again. I'm just glad everyone got out alive."

The Euler house in St. Petersburg, along with many other buildings, was destroyed in the great fire. All of Euler's furniture and books—and many of his mathematical papers—were gone. But some were also saved, and as he said, everything was saved in his mind. The Russian empress Catherine was so impressed with Euler's work that when she heard of the fire she presented him with a new, completely furnished home.

Euler never lost the thrill of new discoveries. On the day of his death he spent the morning calculating how balloons ascend, and the afternoon tracing the orbit of Uranus, a newly discovered planet. After dinner with friends, he relaxed with his pipe and asked for one of his grandsons. Children loved Euler, and he was invigorated by their presence. While playing with the little boy, Euler had a stroke. He took the piece of chalk off the slate beside him, and wrote on the board, "I die." It was the end of a very productive life, but not the end of his influence. His work continues to shape modern mathematics to this very day.

JOSEPH LOUIS LAGRANGE (*zho-SEF loo-EE la-GRAHNZH*), 1736–1813, was a French physicist and mathematician who studied number theory and calculus. A teacher, he helped found two academies of science and made important contributions to the metric system.

The Professor Who Did Not Know

"Let's see now," the disheveled scholar muttered. "If we take the length of the arc and divide it by twelve, we can continue to produce smaller and smaller units of measure."

"Could you demonstrate for me?" asked another committee member.

"Surely. The arc measures 43 units. After dividing by 12 we find that each unit is 3.58333 sub-units. Each of these, after dividing by 12 again, equals .298611 sub-sub-units, or whatever we decide to call them. It's really quite simple."

Joseph Lagrange cleared his throat and blushed slightly. He hated to interrupt the two men but the concept was anything, but simple to him. "May I make a suggestion?" he offered.

"Of course, Joseph, of course."

"Why don't we design a system of measures based on the number ten instead of twelve? Wouldn't it be easier to multiply and divide using ten as a base?"

The others on the Units and Measures Committee squirmed at the suggestion. Twelve had been the standard number for so long. The Egyptians and Greeks had clearly recognized its superiority. But Lagrange was already standing at the head of the table demonstrating how easy it was to measure using a base of ten.

"Notice, gentlemen, that by using 10 a measurement may be written in different units just by moving the decimal point. After all, we have 10 digits, 0 to 9, and our numbers have place values based on 10: the 1s, 10s, 100s, and so forth. Thus, 0.298611 meters becomes 2.98611 decimeters and 29.8611 centimeters and so forth."

Lagrange's colleagues couldn't really argue. As usual, he had taken a difficult situation and made it easy. These men had been searching for one uniform system of measuring length and weight and volume for as long as they could remember. Perhaps Lagrange's suggestion was the breakthrough they needed.

Certainly they needed to do something. Almost every district in France had its own system of measuring and weighing. It was practically impossible to buy or sell fruits and vegetables outside of one's own community. And if anyone tried to buy property in another area, it was hard to tell if the lot was big enough for a home or just large enough for a flagpole.

The first challenge was to find a new, standard unit of length. Ancient peoples had used many nonstandard objects, such as the human arm. Clearly, this would not do for the sophisticated needs of the eighteenth century. The committee, led by Lagrange, decided to determine the length that is one ten-millionth of the distance between the North Pole and the equator. This would be the unit of length. They would call it a meter, from the Greek word "metron," meaning "measure."

Measuring the distance from the North Pole to the equator was another problem. After careful consideration, the French Academy of Sciences authorized a precise measurement of the meridian between Dunkirk, France and Barcelona, Spain. Given these measurements, scientists used astronomical calculations to determine the total length and to find the length of the first meter.

It was the first day of classes at the Ecole Polytechnique. Pierre and Michel beamed with anticipation.

"Aren't we lucky to be a part of this great new school, Pierre?" asked Michel.

"It's the dream of a lifetime for me," Pierre answered. "I still can't believe that I'll get to study under the great Lagrange."

"I can't either. I've heard so much about him, and I've studied his masterpiece, *Analytical Mechanics*, but this will be something else. Do you think we'll be able to understand him?"

"Sh-h-h. We'll soon find out. Here he comes!"

A hush swept through the room. Among the students, Lagrange had a reputation as a mathematical giant. They were surprised when a rather small, timid man entered the room. His pale blue eyes looked out over his new challenge, and he smiled nervously before beginning to lecture. But as Lagrange began to talk, the students' attention was riveted by his clear, systematic explanation of the latest mathematical knowledge.

At lunchtime, Pierre wasn't even hungry. "What do you think, Michel? Have you ever heard anyone like him?"

"He is incredible, Pierre, absolutely incredible. I've never heard anyone make difficult ideas so easy to understand. Some of our old professors tried so hard to impress us with how much they knew. They kept their knowledge to themselves. But did you see how he responded when that fellow in the front row asked his foolish question?"

"Oh, yes," said Pierre. "I was so embarrassed for him! I would never have had the courage to ask anything. He obviously wasn't thinking well today."

"Yes, but did you see what Professor Lagrange did?" Michel asked. "It was as if he crawled inside that student's mind and saw the problem from his perspective. He saw exactly where the confusion was, and how to clear it up."

As the term progressed, Lagrange continued to impress the students with his clear and organized teaching. He was careful never to insult his students, however unprepared they were. Instead, he had a unique ability to see things from their points of view. Few professors of Lagrange's stature were as well-loved and respected as he. His modesty may have touched his students most. He was modest about his achievements and didn't pretend to know everything. In fact, students and fellow scholars admiringly repeated his most famous quotation: "I do not know."

Of course, Lagrange did not use this expression as an excuse for ignorance. Rather, whenever he heard himself say it, he made a mental note to find out all he could about the question. Lagrange was a hard worker, committed to learning. He hadn't started studying mathematics seriously until he was fifteen, but when he was only seventeen he was appointed professor of mathematics at the Royal School of Artillery at Turin, Italy. He taught and wrote, and began to win prizes for his ideas and discoveries.

One of his discoveries answered a question mathematicians had been asking for fifty years: Assume you have a series of different geometric figures. Each has the same perimeter or distance around it. Which figure encloses the maximum area? A method for solving problems such as this one was one of Lagrange's first important achievements.

Later, Lagrange became interested in the earth, sun, and moon. Astronomers had observed that the moon always showed the same face to the earth, and Lagrange wondered why. This led him to discover a mathematical theory explaining the gravitational attraction between these three bodies. The French Academy awarded Lagrange the Grand Prize for his theory when he was only twenty-eight.

Lagrange also proved that every positive integer can be expressed as the sum of four or fewer square numbers (numbers that are the product of a whole number multiplied by itself). For example: $7 = 1 + 1 + 1 + 4$, $34 = 9 + 25$, and $29 = 4 + 9 + 16$. This finding has been especially valuable to those working in *number theory*. Many people believe this was his most significant contribution to mathematics.

Lagrange's influence was beginning to be felt throughout the scientific communities of Europe. King Frederick of Prussia had formed a prestigious college of mathematics in Berlin. Frederick sent this rather impressive invitation to Lagrange: "The greatest king in Europe must have the greatest mathematician in Europe in his court!"

Clearly, Frederick was not as modest as Lagrange, but he was an avid supporter of science and mathematics. Lagrange went to Berlin, where he researched and taught for twenty years. Often he worked too hard and became ill. His doctors refused to take responsibility for him unless he rested and exercised more, but it took the king to get Lagrange to change. King Frederick persuaded Lagrange that life should be lived with "perfect regularity." When he began to think of the mind and body as machines, Lagrange realized he could only expect them to do so much before breaking down. After this, each morning he would write down a reasonable amount to accomplish that day. When he completed his list, he quit until the next day.

Even this strictly disciplined approach did not guarantee happiness. In 1787 King Frederick died. Lagrange accepted Louis XVI's invitation to come to Paris. Louis and the queen, Marie Antoinette, welcomed Lagrange enthusiastically. They gave him an excellent salary, a comfortable apartment in the Louvre, and a chance to teach the best students at the French Academy of Sciences. But Lagrange was exhausted from years of hard work. He surprised everyone who knew his work by saying mathematics was dead. Lagrange was sure that science was the field of the future. He felt he would never study mathematics again.

Attempts to cheer Lagrange out of his depression failed. He studied metaphysics, history of religion, languages, medicine, and botany, but for him the field of mathematics was "finished." In 1789 the violence of the French Revolution shook him out of his lethargy—but it was an unexpected romance that reawakened his love of mathematics.

The bright young daughter of Lemonnier, an astronomer friend of Lagrange's, became attracted to the mathematician. At first Lagrange would not consider a serious relationship with her; after all, she was nearly forty years younger than he. But she persisted and they were married. The marriage turned out to be ideal, and his devoted young wife inspired Lagrange to renew his mathematical work.

Lagrange was quick to praise persons who had encouraged or influenced him. He applauded when Napoleon ordered a tribute to Lagrange's father, still living in Italy. He acknowledged the greatness of Euler. He mourned when the chemist Lavoisier was sentenced to death by guillotine. And just as he recognized those who had affirmed him, he was quick to encourage younger mathematicians.

Once, while teaching at the Ecole Polytechnique, he received an impressive paper from a Monsieur LeBlanc. He couldn't recall a student by that name. After some research, he discovered that the mystery student was really a young woman named Sophie Germain. Only men were allowed at the Ecole, so Sophie had borrowed lecture notes from friends and asked them to smuggle her paper in among theirs. Lagrange went immediately to her home and made her feel like a true mathematician, helping launch her important career.

Even the eleven-year-old Augustin Cauchy, who used to sit in the corner of his father's office in Luxembourg Palace, got an encouraging word from the great mathematician. When Lagrange came to the office on business, young Augustin often showed him his mathematical projects. One day, in front of several important men, Lagrange said, "Someday that little man will surpass all of us, insofar as we are mathematicians."

Cauchy did become a great mathematician, but few historians would say that he surpassed Lagrange. In fact, Lagrange is considered one of the greatest mathematicians of the eighteenth century.

SOPHIE GERMAIN (*so-FEE zhair-MAN*), 1776–1831, was a French mathematician who was particularly interested in number theory and analysis. She won an important prize for formulating a theory of how elastic surfaces vibrate.

Mathematics at Midnight

Sophie lay perfectly still in the darkness. She listened for any sign that her parents were still awake. After what seemed like an hour, she carefully crept out of bed. Wrapping a comforter around her, she tiptoed over to the closet where she had hidden candles inside her shoes. She was sorry to go against her parents' wishes, but it had to be done. She could not wait until morning to finish her calculations.

Candles lit on her table, thirteen-year-old Sophie pulled her icy feet up onto the chair and tucked them under the blanket. She blew on her fingers to keep them from stiffening in the cold. Soon she was so absorbed in her work that she didn't notice her chilly surroundings.

It was all Archimedes's fault. If his story hadn't been so intriguing, maybe Sophie would have stuck to poetry or music. She had read it in her father's library. Sophie shivered whenever she remembered that first spellbinding reading. Archimedes was a brilliant man.

Mathematics and science practically began with his work. But his death—the way he died—*that* was what really gave Sophie chills.

Archimedes had been helping the citizens of Syracuse defend themselves against the Romans. The enemy, under Marcellus, was outraged at Archimedes's amazing inventions. He had built catapults to throw heavy weights at enemy ships. He had designed cranes that hoisted ships from the water and shook them until they cracked. He had used large "burning-glasses," like gigantic magnifying lenses, which focused light on enemy ships until they got so hot they burst into flames. But after three years, Archimedes and the Greeks were conquered.

Marcellus gave strict orders for Archimedes to be taken alive. He had plenty of ways to use such a creative captive. His soldiers found Archimedes absorbed in a geometry problem.

"Rise and follow me!" shouted the soldier at Archimedes's back.

Archimedes was preoccupied with the problem he was working on in the sand. He never even looked up. "Move out of my light," he mumbled. "Can't you see I'm working?"

Without warning, the enraged soldier unsheathed his spear and thrust it through the old man.

Sophie wanted to know what Archimedes had been working on. What could be so engaging, so exciting, that a person would ignore his own impending death? When Sophie learned it was mathematics, she set out to discover how numbers and shapes could be so fascinating.

When Sophie was very young, her parents had welcomed her interest. They allowed her to use her father's library whenever she wished. But soon they decided that she was studying too much. They agreed with the popular notion that "brainwork" was not healthy—

maybe even dangerous—for girls. They told Sophie that she could not study mathematics anymore.

But Sophie would not give up. Night after night she crawled out of bed and studied after everyone else had gone to sleep. Like most parents, Sophie's soon found out. In a desperate attempt to save their daughter, they took away her lamps, hid her clothes at bedtime, and made sure there was no heat in her room. That way she would have to stay under the covers until morning when they could watch her. But Sophie smuggled candles into her room when no one was watching. At night she wrapped herself in her comforter and studied secretly by candlelight.

One morning Sophie's parents discovered her asleep at her desk. Her slate was full of calculations, and the ink was frozen in its well.

"Sophie. Sophie, wake up!"

"Ummm . . . uh . . . Mother, Father?"

"Sophie, haven't we been clear about what we expect of you? Why must you disobey us?" her father implored.

"Oh, Father, I'm so sorry, but I just can't stop," Sophie cried. "These problems are so fascinating! When I work on them I feel like I'm really alive."

"But, Sophie," her mother said softly, "remember, you're a girl. It isn't good for you to fill your mind with numbers."

"Mother, I promise I will stop if I become sick or tired. Can't you see that *not* being able to study this would make me really ill?"

With that her parents gave up. Sophie was allowed to study to her heart's content. Fortunately, her father had an excellent library. As wealthy citizens, the Germain family knew many educated people in Paris and throughout France.

When Sophie was young, however, traveling and visiting were restricted by the political turmoil in France. The French Revolution began in 1789 when she was thirteen, and Paris was an unstable and dangerous city. Often, mobs of people fought in the streets. Sophie's parents shielded her from the fighting and conflict. She eagerly filled her time reading and learning.

One day her friend Pierre came running up to the gate.

"Sophie! Sophie! Have you heard the good news?"

"Calm down, Pierre, and catch your breath."

"This is so exciting!" Pierre exclaimed. A group of scholars have organized a new school, to open next year right here in Paris. They will call it 'Ecole Polytechnique.' Students will come from all of France to study mathematics and science. And I may get to go!"

"That's very nice," Sophie responded dully.

"What's wrong with you? Didn't you hear what I said? Lagrange will be teaching there, and he's the best! Sophie, it's the opportunity of a lifetime!"

"For you, maybe it is," said Sophie. "You forget, Pierre, that I am a girl. I may be eighteen now, but that doesn't change things for a woman. We members of the 'weaker sex' may not attend the school."

"Oh, that's right," Pierre said, subdued. "I'm sorry, Sophie. I forgot you were a girl. In all our studying, I just forgot."

Sophie was right. The Ecole Polytechnique opened in Paris, without women. But Sophie was not easily shut out. She asked her friends to copy lecture notes for her and, at home, studied along with them. She especially liked Professor Lagrange's ideas. When he asked his students to submit papers, she prepared one too and had her friends to smuggle it in among their own. Of course, she knew he wouldn't read one from anyone named "Sophie," so she used a man's name: "Monsieur LeBlanc."

Lagrange looked over all the students' papers. He was especially impressed by Monsieur LeBlanc's. In fact, he requested to meet

Monsieur LeBlanc in person to discuss his paper. When the professor learned his mystery student's true identity, he was shocked—but not upset. He went straight to Sophie's home to congratulate and encourage her. It was one of the most treasured moments of her life.

Still, no universities would admit a woman who wanted to study science and mathematics. Sophie continued to study alone. But after meeting Lagrange, she began to correspond with several scholars and scientists. Usually she used a man's name because some of the prominent men she wrote to refused to take women seriously.

Because Sophie was especially interested in number theory, she became fascinated by the work of Carl Gauss. Gauss was an outstanding German mathematician. He had written an article called *Arithmetic Researches*. Many mathematicians studied it, but few understood everything Gauss was trying to explain. That was the kind of challenge Sophie Germain liked. She wrestled with Gauss's ideas and formulas and discovered some that he hadn't seen. Sophie gathered up her courage and wrote to Gauss. She signed the letter "Monsieur LeBlanc."

Gauss was surprised to get such brilliant feedback from a French mathematician he had never heard of. He welcomed the chance to exchange ideas with an enthusiastic new friend. They corresponded for three years. Gauss never suspected Sophie's true identity.

At this time the French army invaded Germany and took over the town of Hanover, where Gauss lived. Sophie feared for Gauss's safety—perhaps remembering the horrible fate of Archimedes. But what could she do?

"Sophie," sang her mother, interrupting Sophie's studies for the fourth time that afternoon. "Several of General Pernety's commanders are coming for dinner tonight. I hope you will join us at the table."

"Oh, Mother, I'd rather not," Sophie replied. "I never know what to say. I wish I weren't so shy around people."

"Nonsense," said her mother. "You'll be fine."

As the dishes were being cleared from the table after dinner, Sophie suddenly knew what to say to the army commander, and she knew she *had* to say it. The commanders had begun talking about their latest assignment—to join General Pernety himself in Hanover. She saw her chance to help the man who had helped her so much during the past three years.

"Did you say you were going to Hanover?" she asked the men quietly.

"Yes. Tomorrow morning, in fact." The military leaders all looked at Sophie, startled by her sudden interest in their conversation.

"Would you do me a favor?" she continued.

"Of course. Whatever you ask."

Sophie explained, "One of my friends, Monsieur Carl Gauss, lives in Hanover. He is a great mathematician, and not at all political. He is no threat to us—but he might not realize the danger he is in, as a German." Sophie struggled for the words she needed. "Could you ask General Pernety to make sure Monsieur Gauss is safe?"

"Certainly, Mademoiselle Germain. The General has been a friend of your family's for a long time. I'm sure he will be happy to honor your request."

Sophie smiled and relaxed. "Thank you so much."

In Hanover, when General Pernety's men knocked on Gauss's door, he assured them he was fine.

"But why do you ask?" he said.

"Mademoiselle Sophie Germain has requested it."

Gauss was in no position to question the soldiers, but he puzzled all day over the incident. He had never heard of anyone named

Sophie Germain! After several more letters had passed between them, the truth came out. Sophie had no reason to worry; Gauss was just as open-minded about women scholars as Lagrange had been. If anything, he was even more impressed with her work, and respected her as a fellow mathematician. Although the two never met, Gauss helped inform his colleagues of Sophie's talent and accomplishments.

In 1816 mathematicians and scientists around the world heard about Sophie Germain. In that year she won the grand prize from the French Academy for her work on the law of vibrating elastic surfaces. This theory helped to explain and predict the unusual patterns formed by sand or powder on elastic surfaces when they were vibrated. The mathematical formula Sophie wrote helped scientists solve practical problems in sound and building construction. Such studies in elasticity made the construction of the Eiffel Tower possible.

Sophie Germain enjoyed only a brief moment of recognition for a lifetime of dedicated study. The barriers to women in mathematics certainly hampered Germain's development—but they did not prevent her from following her quest.

CARL FRIEDRICH GAUSS (*KARL FREE-drick GOWS*), 1777–1855, was the greatest German mathematician of the nineteenth century. He made contributions to number theory, differential geometry, and statistics. He also studied physics and astronomy, and became famous for successfully predicting the orbit of the asteroid Ceres.

The Teacher Who Learned a Lesson

"Herr Büttner must have had grump porridge for breakfast today, Hans. He's awfully mean," whispered Carl.

"That's nothing new," his friend shrugged.

Just then, their teacher slammed his book down on the front desk and shouted at the class of boys.

"Do I have to thrash you all every day to get you to be quiet and do your work? You boys are the most undisciplined rascals I have ever had to teach. But teach you I will," he continued with fury in his voice. "Yes, today you will learn a lesson!"

Drawing himself up proudly in front of the class, Herr Büttner had everyone's attention. No one dared to whisper or smile or even look at his classmates. When their teacher was angry, he was angry.

"This is the assignment. Listen carefully." Herr Büttner glowered. "You must each add up all the numbers from 1 to 100. When you are finished, you must bring your slate here to my table, and place it face down. Then return to your desk and wait until the rest of the class is finished."

This was not the first time the heartless teacher had given difficult problems; in fact, he specialized in such tactics. He either knew the answers or had a simple formula he could use to find them—but the problems kept the boys busy for hours, giving him free time. He prided himself on being one of the finest teachers in Braunschweig, Germany. It was unfortunate, he thought, that his students did not show him more respect.

But this time something unusual happened. Before Herr Büttner could turn around and sit down on his stool, Carl slipped out of his seat and carefully placed his slate face down on the teacher's desk.

"Young man, are you defying my authority?" the teacher scowled.

"No sir," answered Carl. "I have finished my work."

Herr Büttner scoffed to himself, but decided not to expose his young student's stupidity immediately. Why not wait until the others were finished, and then make a public spectacle of this foolish ten-year-old? He settled back on his stool to plot his strategy.

Much later, Jacob sighed and placed his slate on top of Carl's. Then Hans went up, a pained look on his face, followed by the other boys in the class. Knowing they would not be excused until everyone had finished, some of the slower boys just guessed to get it over with.

At last it was Herr Büttner 's opportunity to teach Carl a lesson. His slate was on the bottom of the pile. Herr Büttner turned over the top slate and declared, "Incorrect." The next slate was also wrong, as was the next and the next. At last there was only one slate left—that of the student who had so brashly delivered it in only a few seconds.

The class watched in suspense as Herr Büttner slowly and deliberately turned over Carl's slate. To his amazement, there was only one number on the slate—5,050. It was the correct answer! How could Carl have done it? For once, the teacher was shocked into silence. His face turned white. He couldn't say a word, except "Class dismissed."

That evening on his way home, Carl stopped by his uncle Friedrich's tapestry shop. He couldn't resist telling his uncle what had happened at school.

"That's wonderful, Carl," laughed Uncle Friedrich, as he pictured the humiliated schoolmaster. "I am very proud of you!"

"Thank you. I wish Papa would be proud of me, too."

"Well, Carl, you mustn't feel too bad about that. Your father is a good, hardworking man. He never had an education, so he doesn't see the use of it. Maybe someday he'll understand that not every boy wants to be a bricklayer or a gardener. Be thankful your mother and I were raised differently. Speaking of your mother, hadn't you better be getting home?"

"I guess you're right, Uncle," Carl said. "Maybe I'll see you tomorrow."

"Say, Carl, before you go, how *did* you solve that problem?"

"It was easy," Carl explained. "I saw that $1 + 100 = 101$, $2 + 99 = 101$, and $3 + 98 = 101$. I could tell that if you add up all the numbers from 1 to 100, you can find 50 pairs of numbers that each add up to 101. So 50 times 101 would be the answer. You could have done it yourself!"

The Gauss family was not wealthy. In fact, compared to the families of most boys in Carl's school, they were downright poor. But encouragement is often more valuable than money or fancy clothes, and Carl's mother was a great encourager. She was a strong woman with a good sense of humor. Though she had little education, she was intelligent and wanted her children to do their best.

Carl didn't need much motivating—not where numbers were concerned. Once, before he was three years old, Carl overheard his father figuring out his workers' pay. "Excuse me, Papa, but I think you made a mistake in your reckoning," little Carl said.

When he looked at his columns again, Mr. Gauss saw that his son was right! He had solved the problem in his head. Later, as an adult, Carl Gauss sometimes joked that he could "reckon"—do arithmetic—before he could talk. Perhaps he was right.

To those who knew him it was obvious that Carl Friedrich Gauss was a genius. But his father never admitted it, and never agreed to Carl's going to school. Fortunately his mother and her brother Friedrich knew it was important. And even the stern Herr Büttner played a part in helping Gauss learn.

Several weeks after Carl had outwitted him, Büttner brought Carl a gift—the best textbook on arithmetic that was available. And he confessed that there was nothing else he could teach Carl; Carl must have a private tutor.

At that time, the young mathematician Johann Bartels was working in Braunschweig. Although he was only seventeen years old, he was considered brilliant. Carl and Johann began to study together and share ideas about mathematics. For Carl, it was a very invigorating time.

"Carl, there is someone who wants to meet you," announced Johann one day.

"Well, introduce me," said Carl.

"But this isn't just anyone. It's the Duke of Brunswick."

"The Duke himself?" asked Carl. "You must be teasing me!"

"Not this time. Last night my family and I were invited to a party for some friends of the Duke, and he was there," Johann explained. "Some of us got to talking about ideas, about arithmetic and astronomy and other exciting subjects. Then the Duke joined us. He asked who Germany's leading thinkers would be—you know, like he was playing a game, except he really wanted to know."

"You're not making this up, are you?" Carl asked suspiciously.

"No, Carl, I'm completely earnest. The Duke wants to meet you as soon as possible."

Carl was only fourteen and was shy. Meeting Carl Wilhelm Ferdinand, Duke of Brunswick, was the most frightening thing that had ever happened to him. But it turned out to be the luckiest. The Duke was so impressed with young Carl that he offered to pay all his expenses at Caroline College. This famous school helped prepare students to attend university. Carl could never have afforded to go on his own. However, with the Duke's support and his mother's encouragement, he went.

At college, Gauss studied all sorts of subjects. He loved literature and learned several languages. His photographic memory certainly came in handy studying vocabulary lists! But he never outgrew his love of mathematics. He knew he would have to choose one subject as a major area for study. What should it be?

Thanks to the Duke of Brunswick, Gauss was able to study at the University of Göttingen. There, on the day before his nineteenth birthday, he made a remarkable discovery. He found that a regular polygon with 17 sides could be drawn using just a compass and straightedge. For over 2,000 years, mathematicians had believed that this was impossible. Usually quiet and humble, Gauss was openly proud of this discovery. He immediately decided to devote his life to mathematics. On that very day he began to keep a secret science diary in which he wrote down ideas, questions, problems, and solutions.

Many of Gauss's ideas were not discovered until long after his death, when his secret diary was examined. He was a perfectionist and refused to publish theories that were not complete and polished. He simply did not have time to share everything he learned.

One afternoon, a friend of Gauss's visited the famous mathematician. Over a cup of tea they shared their latest discoveries. Gauss showed his friend the formulas in his secret notebook, and the friend was astounded.

"Why haven't you shared this with other scientists and mathematicians? You have some marvelous insights here."

Gauss turned his piercing blue eyes towards his friend, and lifting one eyebrow, smiled.

"I will tell you, my friend," he said. "A cathedral is not a cathedral until the last piece of scaffolding is removed."

After Gauss died, the King of Hanover ordered a medal to be prepared in his honor. On it was inscribed "The Prince of

Mathematics." Even today, scholars everywhere consider Gauss, along with Archimedes and Newton, as one of the three greatest mathematicians who ever lived.

EVARISTE GALOIS (*ay-va-REEST gahl-WAH*), 1811–1832, was a French mathematician. He made major contributions to several branches of mathematics, including algebra, number theory, and group theory.

"Don't Let My Life Be Wasted!"

Evariste Galois took a deep breath. The fragrance of the wisteria vines in the park strengthened him as he walked towards home. Spring was a time for new beginnings, he thought. Maybe his luck would improve. If he could just put on a little weight to make up for what he'd lost in prison; then he'd have energy to plan his future. Deep in thought, Galois did not notice the two men lurking in the shadows of his building. Just as he was about to open his door, they stepped in front of him.

"You're Evariste Galois, aren't you?"

"Yes. Yes, I am. Who are you? What do you want?"

"Don't play dumb with me!" The taller man lunged closer to Galois so that the young mathematician could smell his foul breath. "You're trying to steal my Eve, aren't you?"

"Never!" shouted Galois. "Why should I try to steal something of no worth?"

"That does it," snarled the bully. "There is only one way to settle a question of honor. We will duel with pistols tomorrow morning at sunrise. Meet me at the fountain on the Rue Cochin—or else."

"But listen," stammered Galois. "I have no interest in these things. I have work to do. I'm a mathematician, not a petty streetfighter!"

"You think this is petty, eh? You think I'm petty too, don't you? Well, some of us are getting tired of your interfering around here. You may as well say goodbye to your numbers—whether you show up tomorrow morning or not. But if honor means anything to you, if you have any pride, you'd better be there at sunrise."

Galois staggered up the stairs to his room. His heart was pounding. He didn't know what to make of the threats. Something told him this was more than a fight over a girl. The two thugs looked vaguely familiar. Had he seen them on the edge of the crowd at the political rally last week? He couldn't be sure.

One thing *was* sure: he would have to duel in the morning. There was no escaping such a challenge. Refusal to duel was the worst form of cowardice. But what a shame to die for such an unworthy cause! He would have been proud to die for his country in the war. He would have been willing to die for virtue or for principles he believed in. But to die over a girl he barely knew and didn't care for was a terrible waste.

Waste. The word echoed in Galois's mind. So much of his life could be described as a waste. As a boy he'd had boundless enthusiasm and energy, but it had been wasted over and over until an end like this seemed almost fitting.

Galois sank into a worn chair and allowed the painful memories to parade through his mind. None of it could be blamed on his parents. They were fine people, he reflected. His mother was a strong woman of character. She came from a family of judges and had taught Galois to hate injustice. Actually, she had taught him almost every subject until he turned twelve and started attending school. His father had contributed, too. He was headmaster of the boarding school in their village. Monsieur Galois's hobby was making up rhymes, mostly for fun. Evariste smiled in spite of himself as he remembered mimicking his father's verses. Like his wife, Nicolas Galois was an ardent lover of liberty. He spoke out freely against the royalty's oppression of the people. A cultivated, intellectual man, he served his village as mayor until . . . Galois hung his head and shuddered as he remembered that awful day. Overwhelmed by the attacks against him, his father had slipped into Paris and killed himself.

Young Evariste had had problems even before that. He remembered the chills he felt when he and his mother first looked upon Louis-le-Grand, the school he entered at age twelve. The dismal gray buildings had bars on the windows and massive grilled gates. It looked more like a prison than a school. Inside, the mood was the same. Harsh, domineering teachers were not successful at motivating Evariste to work hard. Instead, he rebelled against their treatment. Soon he refused to study or do his assignments. They demoted him, putting him in a lower grade. Some of the teachers thought he was just plain stupid.

Galois loved learning, but he struggled with the textbooks his teachers made him use. He wanted to read the original works of great thinkers—not some childish version of their discoveries. Once he got a copy of the mathematician Legendre's work on geometry. He read it cover to cover like other boys might read a good mystery.

Galois liked to do mathematics problems in his head. This caused all sorts of trouble. His teachers, of course, wanted to see his calculations on paper. He soon gained a reputation as a difficult, argumentative student.

Most of all, Galois wanted to attend the prestigious Ecole Polytechnique in Paris. At this school, encouraged by some of the greatest living scholars, he knew he could develop his love of mathematics. He had been nervous when he went to take the exams, but they had not been difficult for him. What a shocking disappointment it was to learn that he had not passed the entrance tests. Even there, the examiners wanted to see all of Galois's steps methodically scratched on the paper—but he had done the work in his head.

It took a long time to get over the unjust test results. But Galois was still young, and he could try other ways to gain admission to the Ecole Polytechnique. When he was seventeen, Galois was very encouraged when Professor Louis-Paul-Emile Richard arrived at his school. Professor Richard was a great teacher and saw immediately that Galois was a genius. He used Galois's work as teaching outlines for the rest of the class. He also urged the bright young student to collect his discoveries and send them to the French Academy, France's finest group of scholars.

Galois accepted the challenge and prepared a paper about his discoveries. He sent it to Augustin-Louis Cauchy, a professor at the Ecole Polytechnique. Cauchy was a famous mathematician himself. However, he must have been either careless or closed-minded about young people, because he never read Galois's work—in fact, he lost it.

Later, Galois decided to take the Ecole Polytechnique entrance test again. Only two tries were allowed, and he'd already tried once. This time the examiners began with their minds set against Galois. They had heard that he was very intelligent, but they thought he should be more humble. Perhaps they were afraid that one day he would replace them. During the oral part of the examination, they began to taunt him, ridiculing his work and scoffing at his answers. Suddenly, in a moment of frustration, Galois grabbed an eraser and hurled it at one of the examiners, hitting him in the face. That was the end of his hopes for admission to the best school of mathematics in Europe.

Finally, when he was nineteen, Galois decided to go to the university. He worked unappreciated and alone, but he produced some valuable papers on algebra. One of the most important functions of algebra is to solve *equations*. Galois discovered which equations could be solved using algebra and which could not.

In a moment of optimism, Galois decided to submit his work to the Academy of Sciences in competition for the Grand Prize in Mathematics. The secretary received Galois's work, but before he could read it, he died. When officials went to his office to retrieve Galois's papers, they had mysteriously disappeared. No one ever found out what happened to his work. Galois's friends suspected that someone jealous of Galois's monumental discovery had "misplaced" the papers deliberately.

Galois could have coped with normal disappointments, but so many setbacks took their toll on him. Bitterness filled him. He began to distrust all teachers and all institutions. He tried starting his own school, but no one enrolled. Then, because he wanted to fight injustice, he got involved in politics. He joined the Republicans, a forbidden radical group. They spoke out for justice, especially for the poor, and for freedom of the press. They wanted a better standard of living for the common people, instead of for the wealthy few.

One night in 1831, over 200 Republicans gathered together for a banquet. While they enjoyed their meal, several of the young men stood to offer toasts, to arouse spirit and enthusiasm for the tasks ahead.

Galois was the second to offer a toast.

"Here's to Louis Philippe!" he mocked. The crowd roared at Galois's gesture—they knew he felt no love for the king. But several in the audience did not laugh. They were spies for the king, quietly watching to make sure the gathering did not pose a serious threat. When Galois stood, they sat up straight. Like arrows, their eyes focused on Galois's left hand. As he raised his wine glass in his right hand, his left hand clutched an open knife.

The next morning, before Galois awakened, there was a sharp knock at his door.

"Galois, you're under arrest."

"Under arrest?" he protested. "For what?"

"You have threatened the life of the king. You must be imprisoned until trial. Come with us."

Eventually, Galois was acquitted of the charges. The knife, he explained, was just for cutting his meat. But a month later he was arrested again, this time for being a dangerous radical—but the charges were hard to prove. Finally the ruling party charged Galois with wearing a uniform when the National Guard he served no longer existed. For that he spent six months in jail.

Conditions in jail were not too uncomfortable. Galois used his time to renew his interest in mathematics. The other inmates constantly teased him because he refused to waste his days getting drunk as they did. He wanted to keep his head clear so he could think and write. Finally, he was released on parole and hoped to begin a new life.

It must have been too good to be true, thought Galois. Suddenly he heard the tower clock chime. He looked out his window. The sky was still black, but it was long past midnight.

"Time is running out," he said aloud. "I have much to do before sunrise."

Feverishly, Galois looked through the papers on his desk. He collected his current projects and sorted them into stacks. Then he began a letter to his friend Auguste Chevalier, describing what he considered his most important discovery: the lost manuscript on the algebraic solution of equations. "Eventually," he wrote, "I hope some people will find it useful to decipher this mess." Galois asked Chevalier to try to get the great mathematicians Jacobi and Gauss to evaluate his work. In silence, except for the ticking of the clock, he hurriedly went over his papers that last night. He scribbled in the margins, "There are a few things to be completed in this proof," or "I do not have time to finish this." All night long Galois labored over his desk in anguished frustration at having to leave so much work undone.

As the sky slowly began to lighten, Galois wrote another letter "To All Young Republicans." He explained that honor required him to go to the duel. His last request was: "Preserve my memory, since fate has not given me life enough for my country to know my name."

Morning came quickly. At the appointed time and place, just before sunrise, Galois was ready. He and his opponent picked up their pistols. As his foe's companion counted, they paced 25 steps in opposite directions, turned, and fired. Galois went down, shot through the intestines. He lay unattended on the street until 9:00 a.m., when a passing peasant picked him up and took him to the hospital. He died the next day after consoling his younger brother, saying "Do not cry. I need all my courage to die at twenty."

The death of Evariste Galois was a terrible waste. If he had known that his work would make a significant contribution to mathematics, perhaps Galois would have felt that his life had had meaning. His discoveries are considered some of the most original mathematical ideas of the nineteenth century. And his name is well known—not just among young radicals in France, but to mathematicians around the world.

AMALIE EMMY NOETHER (*NUR-ter*), 1882–1935, was a German mathematician whose work vitally affected the development of modern algebra.

Life on an Obstacle Course

"Now, Emmy, watch carefully while I stir these eggs into the rest of the batter. You must be very careful to fold the beaten eggs in gently, or the cake will fall flat in the oven."

"I see, Mother," said Emmy automatically.

"Yes, but are you really paying attention?"

"I'm doing my best, Mother."

"Thank you. That's all I can ask of you." Her mother sighed. "Now go and finish dusting the dining room. Some of your father's colleagues will be here for dinner. And don't bother Papa."

Frau Noether went about her baking while her daughter Emmy obediently went to get a cloth for dusting.

The aroma of soup and freshly baked bread mingled with the sweet smell of the cake baking. Frau Noether rushed around the house, making last-minute preparations for her guests. As she walked into the dining room, she stopped with a gasp. The table was so dusty, one could—could—why, one could do mathematics problems on it!

"Emmy," she wailed in a high-pitched voice. She bustled through the house until she found the source of her frustration.

"I should have known I'd find you here," she scolded in exasperation. "Emmy, how many times do I have to tell you to stay away from your father and concentrate on your household duties?"

Emmy stood shamefaced, the clean dustcloth hanging from her hand. "I'm sorry, Mother. Father asked me to get him a fresh pencil, and when I brought it in I thought I'd take just a minute to see what he was working on. Then he started explaining things to me, and then . . . "

"Never mind with the excuses," her mother interrupted. "I've heard them all before! Just hurry in and dust the dining room right now."

Emmy's father had been sheepishly quiet, knowing that he was somewhat to blame for his daughter's delinquency. But now he took off his glasses and smiled at his wife.

"You know, Ida, there's something special about Emmy. Maybe it's time we recognized it. She catches on so quickly; I wish some of my students at the university were as bright. Now don't tell anyone I compared a fourteen-year-old girl to them, but it's true."

"It may be true, Max, but that doesn't change reality," his wife answered. "There's no place for a girl in mathematics. She must learn to run a house and to entertain. She should be thinking about what she will wear to the dance next month. That is much more practical for a girl. What she wants is just not normal. Society will never accept her."

Emmy's father shook his head. "I know you're right, but some things can't be stopped. I think it would be a pitiful waste to try to stop Emmy. She would much rather do mathematics than manage a household, and you know she's better at it anyway."

Ida Noether smiled in spite of herself. "That's certainly true. And since there's no one to help me, I must quit talking and go get ready for our guests."

Emmy was a good girl, and both her parents were proud of her. She did well at the school for girls she attended, and she practiced piano until she could play with ease. She learned all about how to manage a house and act polite at dances. By the time she was eighteen, she was so good at French and English that she passed an exam allowing her to teach both languages in secondary school.

But her heart wasn't in it. What she really wanted to study was mathematics. Perhaps it was her father's influence. He taught mathematics at the University of Erlangen and often came home still excited from his classes. At home, he loved to gather Emmy and her three younger brothers around him and explain complicated ideas in language that his children could understand. He was a good teacher. Emmy and her brother Fritz were especially fascinated with their father's ideas about algebra.

Frau Noether was right: Germany was not ready for a young woman who wanted to study mathematics. At the university in Erlangen, women were not welcome. Sometimes a professor would allow a woman to sit in on a lecture, but women could not enroll. Fortunately for Emmy, her parents supported her ambition and arranged for a tutor to teach her mathematics. She was an energetic and disciplined student. By 1902, when the university decided to admit women, Emmy was ready.

Emmy was the only woman enrolled in mathematics. She concentrated on doing her best work and quickly distinguished herself as a creative scholar. She amazed her fellow students and teachers with her capacity to see the larger concepts underlying mathematical processes. In 1907 Emmy passed the final examination for the doctoral degree in mathematics with high honors.

Getting the education she wanted was a struggle—but Emmy's battle was not over. While the universities were beginning to admit women as students, they would not consider women as professors. How was Noether to support herself? Fortunately, her family came to the rescue. She lived at home for eight years and worked at the university—without pay. Her father, who had had polio as a child, became increasingly handicapped. Noether often taught his classes as a substitute teacher.

After Noether's father retired and her mother died, she moved to the city of Göttingen. At the university there, David Hilbert and Felix Klein were working on Einstein's theory of relativity. This theory describes the relationship between energy, mass, and the speed of light. They had invited Noether to join their small research group, and were enthusiastic about what she could contribute. They worked hard to get the university to hire her. Hilbert even appealed to the University Senate—the governing body of the entire university. When they refused his pleas, he angrily scolded his colleagues for using Noether's gender as an excuse not to hire her. "This is a university," he railed, "not a bathing establishment!"

Gradually, the university grew to respect Emmy Noether as a mathematician and a woman. After several years she was given a modest salary, but the reputation she helped build for Göttingen far outweighed her salary. She published papers and was invited to speak in several countries. Throughout Europe and the United States, mathematicians acknowledged that this woman was changing the way they understood algebra. She had a unique ability to work with abstract concepts. She could visualize complex connections and help others see them, too.

At Göttingen, Noether lived a quiet life. She never married; her first and last love was mathematics. But many people loved her. She was kind and friendly, but her friends knew they could depend on her to be frank with them. Students enjoyed hovering around her. A Noether course was never boring; she preferred an informal classroom to a stiff lecture. Although her classes were stimulating, they were not easy. Noether expected her students to work hard and to channel their energy into thinking. She taught them to find a problem's underlying structure as the key to solving it.

By 1933 Emmy Noether had achieved many of her life goals. She was employed and respected as a professor. She was privileged to work with many of the finest scholars in Europe. And she had the freedom to explore mathematical ideas to her heart's content. All of that changed when Adolf Hitler and the National Socialist Party came to power. In 1933, determined to maintain absolute control—even over ideas—they placed Emmy and many of her colleagues "on leave until further notice."

Noether remained calm and courageous. Her friends marveled at her lack of concern for her self; more than anything, she wanted world peace. But she had three strikes against her: she was an intellectual woman, she was Jewish, and she was politically liberal. It was clear that Noether would have to leave the country.

Bryn Mawr College near Philadelphia offered Noether a "visiting professorship." Although she missed Germany, Noether thoroughly enjoyed her days at Bryn Mawr. For the first time in her career, she received a decent salary. Most important to her, though, was her relationship with students. She loved to walk and often took students with her for a Saturday afternoon jaunt. The students teased that she invited them to protect her: she became so absorbed in talking about mathematics that she'd forget all about the traffic.

While she was at Bryn Mawr, Noether also worked at the Institute for Advanced Studies at Princeton University. Albert Einstein and Hermann Weyl were there at the same time, and the three became a team of common admirers. Noether's studies on abstract rings and ideal theory were important to the development of modern algebra. She showed mathematicians how to build general theories that would apply to many problems.

In 1935 Emmy Noether died unexpectedly from complications of routine surgery. The fact that she was at the peak of her career made her death all the more tragic. Many gathered to pay her respect, and to offer tributes to her contributions to mathematics.

One such person was Einstein, whose words appeared in the *New York Times*: "In the judgment of the most competent living mathematicians, Fraülein Noether was the most significant creative mathematical genius thus far produced since the higher education of women began . . . "

Jean Dieudonne, the eminent French mathematician, said Emmy Noether was "by far the best woman mathematician of all time—one of the greatest mathematicians (male or female) of the twentieth century."

Certainly, Emmy Noether's contribution to mathematics cannot be challenged. But she made another contribution to human history: she showed that following one's dream—and standing up to society's opposition—can lead to great achievement and satisfaction. If Noether had her way, both men and women would be encouraged to do just that.

SRINIVASA RAMANUJAN (*shree-ni-VA-sa rah-MAH-nuh-jun*), 1887–1920, was an Indian mathematician who, with very little education or training, made remarkable discoveries in mathematics.

Numbers Were His Greatest Treasure

The chickens squawked and flapped their wings to dodge the barefooted boy. He darted down the dusty street, almost upsetting a large basket of tea leaves an old farmer was carrying on his shoulder. Finally, he scurried around the corner and into the house.

"Mother! Mother! Guess what!" he said breathlessly.

"Slow down, son. Speak with respect."

"I'm sorry, Mother, but guess what!"

"What, son?" she answered.

"I won the prize in the mathematics contest again! My answer was right! Do you think this means that I'm really good in mathematics? Do you think I'll be famous someday? Do you think so, Mother?"

Ramanujan's mother smiled at him and patted him on the back. "Oh, I'm sure you are very good, Srinivasa. But I can't say if you will be famous. Perhaps there are more important things in this world than being famous."

"Perhaps," mumbled her son, looking down. Lost in thoughts about fame, Ramanujan forgot to show his mother the prize he had won. It was a book of Wordsworth's poetry. Poetry was all right, but to this young boy, there was more beauty and meaning in numbers than in words.

While Srinivasa began his after-school chores, his mother started preparing the evening meal for her family and the high school students who boarded with them. Their home was small—really just a room with a kitchen tacked on—so there was very little private space. Somehow, Srinivasa always found a spot to do his mathematics. His mother chuckled as she thought of his enthusiasm for numbers.

The Ramanujan family was poor, but they had many reasons to be thankful. Srinivasa's mother remembered how she and her husband had wished for a son. They feared they would never have children. Finally, her father had gone to pray for a grandchild at the shrine of the goddess Namagiri. Srinivasa's mother was sure the goddess had answered that prayer. Sometimes she felt that the angels still looked over this special child and even whispered in his ear. How else could he know so much about numbers?

Srinivasa was a good student. He respected his teachers and tried hard in every subject. But he was shy, and speaking was difficult for him. The words got all tangled up in his mouth when he tried to talk, so usually he remained silent.

The only subject Ramanujan found easy to talk about was mathematics. Even as a child, he enjoyed reciting formulas to his friends at school. His teachers and school administrators soon realized that he had unusual ability in mathematics. At the age of seven he was awarded a scholarship to the Kumbakonam Town High School. The scholarship assured his family that in spite of their poverty, he would get an education.

In southern India at that time, few books were available for persons who wanted to study on their own. When Ramanujan was twelve years old, a book in the arms of an older student caught his eye.

"Excuse me, please," Ramanujan stammered. "Could I look for just a moment at the book you're carrying?"

"Which one do you mean?" the student asked.

"That one entitled *Plane Trigonometry*." Ramanujan waited expectantly.

"This book is much too difficult for a child like you to understand," the student responded impatiently. "I can't even figure out what it says."

Ramanujan looked so dejected the student felt sorry for him. "All right, if it means so much to you, take it. Keep it for a week and then bring it back to me. As I said, it isn't doing me any good anyway."

Elated with this opportunity, Ramanujan carefully tucked the book into his coat and ran home. In just a few short days he had read and mastered all the material that the older student had found so confusing. This book and one other book that he borrowed from a library were the only written sources of mathematics he ever saw in India.

At the Government College in Kumbakonam, Ramanujan quickly distinguished himself in mathematics. One day he watched as his algebra teacher slid two portable blackboards back and forth across the front of the room. The solution required ten or eleven steps; it could never all fit on one board. Ramanujan grew impatient. Finally he raised his hand and requested permission to show an alternate solution. His answer was completely right, required only four steps, and was much easier for the class to understand. This was Ramanujan's pattern: he had a unique way of making complex problems simpler.

There was one problem, however, that Ramanujan could not solve. He could not discipline himself to study history, English, or physiology. In fact, when he should have concentrated on those classes, he was often doing mathematics. Finally, he failed so many other courses that he lost his scholarship and had to leave the college. After this happened twice, Ramanujan gave up the idea of college and dedicated himself to working independently on the mathematics he loved so much.

When Ramanujan was twenty-two years old he married Srimathi Janaki. For a while, Ramanchandra Rao, a wealthy man who was impressed by Ramanujan's mathematical discoveries, supported the couple. He was happy to give the mathematician money for food and supplies so he could concentrate on mathematics. But Ramanujan began to feel guilty accepting money without really working for it. He took seriously his responsibility to provide for his family, so he got a job as a clerk.

After working all day at the Madras Port Trust, Ramanujan would rush home to do mathematics problems. Sometimes he carried scrap wrapping paper from the office to use for his calculations. Paper was expensive; usually Ramanujan worked on a slate. When he was excited by a problem he would work very rapidly, doing his calculations in chalk, erasing them with his elbow, and then filling the slate again. Often, he recorded only the final result—making it difficult for later mathematicians to follow his thinking process.

At home, Ramanujan liked to work lying on a cot. In the stifling Indian heat he would work out on the veranda. Once he started his calculations, he did not like to stop for any reason. His wife and his mother, who lived with the young couple according to custom, would prepare his food and often feed him while he worked. Sometimes he would work until 6 a.m., force himself to sleep for two hours, and then get up and go to work.

Fortunately, Ramanujan's employers were sympathetic and encouraging to him. They recognized his talent and suggested he write to English mathematicians about his work. Ramanujan was reluctant. What if no one understood what he was doing? Would it be worth the effort to explain? Finally, Ramanujan agreed to try. He sent a letter to two famous English mathematicians, enclosing sheets of equations and a brief explanation. They returned his work with no comment.

But Ramanujan would not give up. He sent another batch of papers with a letter to Godfrey Hardy at Cambridge University. Hardy was just about to throw away the scribbled sheets when an equation caught his eye. These were not typical solutions to problems; this was the work of an unusual and brilliant mathematician. Hardy immediately wrote back to Ramanujan and offered him a scholarship—all expenses paid—to study at Trinity College.

Deciding to go to England was very difficult for Ramanujan. He had traveled very little, and he was afraid his English wouldn't be adequate. Then there was the question of food: he was a strict vegetarian. Could he find enough fruits, grains, and vegetables there for a healthy diet? But probably the greatest obstacle to travel was his religion. In India, people are divided into groups or *castes*, each with its own rules. Ramanujan and his family belonged to the Brahmin caste; they observed the customs of Hindu religion and culture faithfully. For Brahmins, overseas travel broke the caste's rules. Anyone who had crossed the water would not be allowed to attend Brahmin weddings or funerals.

Ramanujan's mother was a strong-willed woman. She made up her mind that her son would never go to England. The University of Madras in India had offered him a scholarship and she saw no reason for him to leave. The case was closed—until one morning when something very unusual happened.

"Srinivasa, come here!" Ramanujan's mother called from her bed.

It was early morning. Ramanujan was getting ready for work. But he was devoted to his mother, and her voice was filled with urgency.

"What is it, mother? Is something wrong? Are you ill?" Ramanujan bent over her bed.

"No, no. I'm fine, but I just had the strangest dream, and you must listen to me and obey. I dreamt of a great hall, with high ceilings and ornate paintings. You were there, with many others— all Europeans. And then the goddess Namagiri looked right at me and warned me to stay out of your way." She paused and pointed her finger at him. "You must be given freedom to become what you are destined to be."

Ramanujan looked at his mother, stunned. "Perhaps you are not well, Mother. It's only a dream, isn't it?"

As he spoke he knew the answer. If the goddess had spoken to his mother, there was only one thing to do. Soon he was packing for England.

Just before Ramanujan left for England, he sent his mother and wife to a nearby town. He did not want them to see his final preparations. In England things would be very different, and Ramanujan didn't want to stand out. He cut his hair and traded his turban for a hat. He bought a European suit and put on socks and shoes.

The journey to England by ship was difficult. Ramanujan was nervous. But when he arrived, Hardy and others at Trinity College made Ramanujan feel welcome. There was no doubt about his mathematical genius. He eagerly worked with the British mathematicians, who were in awe of his accomplishments. Hardy became his closest friend and colleague in England. The two of them collaborated on many articles and published them in European journals.

Hardy felt privileged to work with Ramanujan, but he never fully understood how Ramanujan did mathematics. The Indian had not had much training; he seemed to depend on insight and intuition. His mathematical signs and symbols were creative, but other mathematicians had no idea what they meant. Hardy's task was to help Ramanujan learn standard forms of writing equations and proofs.

One of Ramanujan and Hardy's most important projects is called partitioning. Their challenge was to find out how many ways an integer can be expressed as the sum of other integers. For example, the number 4 can be expressed as the sum of 1 + 3, 1 + 1 + 2, 1 + 1 + 1 + 1, 2 + 2, or 4 itself, for a total of five ways.

But as numbers increase, the problem becomes more complex. The number 200, for instance, may be partitioned nearly four trillion ways. The notion of being able to calculate the number of partitions in a large number was considered ridiculous—before Ramanujan. But with Hardy's assistance, the Indian genius came up with a formula to do it.

Ramanujan rarely celebrated when he made important discoveries—he didn't have time for such frivolity. But neither he nor Hardy realized how significant his discoveries were. His formulas for partitioning, for example, are vitally important to physicists working with *superstrings*. (Modern physicists believe that tiny particles in the universe are made up of superstrings—twisted bits of matter so small it is hard to imagine them.) Much of Ramanujan's other work could not be fully appreciated until the development of computers. He devised solutions to mathematical problems he could have known nothing about.

One of Ramanujan's most influential accomplishments was discovering simple but accurate ways of approximating the value of *pi*. Pi is the ratio of the circumference of a circle to its diameter. Mathematicians had been trying to figure out its value for centuries. Archimedes in about 250 B.C. and Newton in the seventeenth century made significant progress on this question. But even high-speed computers could not calculate *pi* to the accuracy of millions of decimal places without Ramanujan's formulas.

Although living in England was intellectually stimulating for Ramanujan, the adjustment was difficult. English culture was very different from life in India. He had left his young wife behind, so he had to take care of his personal needs himself. Meals were the biggest problem. No restaurants prepared vegetarian foods the way he enjoyed them, so Ramanujan sent for supplies from India. Cooking was not that hard, but Ramanujan often became so absorbed in his work that he forgot to eat. He didn't sleep regularly, either. Sometimes he would work for thirty-six hours, and finally collapse in fatigue.

These poor health habits, plus the damp and chilly English weather, finally caught up with Ramanujan. About three years after arriving in England, Ramanujan became ill with a mysterious illness. Some doctors thought he had tuberculosis. Others recognized the symptoms of a severe vitamin deficiency. But no one knew how to help him. He tried and failed to find a cure in several nursing homes and hospitals. Finally, after six years in England, Ramanujan returned to India. He hoped that going back to his native climate where someone could care for him might restore his health.

Being home again made Ramanujan feel better. He told his wife that he should have taken her to England—perhaps then he would not have become ill. Although he was not healthy, Ramanujan soon resumed his mathematical exploration, collecting ideas on papers and depositing them in an old leather trunk he kept under his bed.

But Ramanujan's health did not improve. He became progressively weaker. Ramanujan died a year after returning to India. He was only thirty-two years old. In spite of his brief life, he had attained a worldwide reputation. In 1918 he had been elected Fellow of the Royal Society of London and Fellow of Trinity College. He was the first Indian to be awarded either honor. Hardy and the others who had known Ramanujan at Cambridge were deeply grieved to hear of his death.

One of the stories Hardy used to tell about Ramanujan provides a clue to his mathematical greatness. Once when Ramanujan was very ill—near death—Hardy went to visit him in the hospital. Hardy didn't know what to say when he saw Ramanujan lying so still. He started the conversation awkwardly: "Ahem . . . I came over here to see you in a taxi," Hardy stammered. "It was taxi number 1729."

Ramanujan smiled at his friend, his eyes shining.

"Taxi number 1729," Hardy repeated. "Rather a dull number, wouldn't you say?"

Ramanujan propped himself up in the bed and spoke in a strong voice. "No, Hardy, not at all. In fact, 1729 is a very interesting number. It is the smallest number that can be expressed as the sum of two cubes in two different ways."

Hardy was stunned. Ramanujan, self-taught and unpredictable, had an uncanny ability with numbers. How could one describe it? It seemed as if numbers, including the number 1729, were Ramanujan's personal friends. He remembered their characteristics the way one might remember a friend's birth date or favorite color. He treated them with reverence and respect: they were his greatest treasure.

History of Mathematics
Resource List

◆

Aaboe, Asger. *Episodes from the Early History of Mathematics.* Washington, D.C.: Mathematical Association of America, 1964.

Abbott, David. *The Biographical Dictionary of Scientists: Mathematicians.* New York: Peter Bedrick Books, 1986.

Ball, W.W. Rouse. *A Short Account of the History of Mathematics.* New York: Dover Publications, Inc., 1960.

Beckman, Petr. *A History of Pi.* New York: St. Martin's Press, 1971.

Bell, E.T. *Men of Mathematics.* New York: Simon & Schuster, 1937.

Bixby, William. *The Universe of Galileo and Newton.* New York: American Heritage, 1964; distributed by Harper & Row.

Boyer, Carl B. and Uta Merzbach. *A History of Mathematics.* New York: John Wiley & Sons, Inc., 1989.

Burton, David M. *The History of Mathematics.* Boston: Allyn & Bacon, Inc., 1985.

Cajori, Florian. *A History of Mathematics.* New York: Chelsea, 1985.

———. *History of Mathematical Notations.* Vols. 1 & 2. Chicago: Open Court, 1929.

Diggins, Julia. *String, Straightedge and Shadow: The Story of Geometry*. New York: Viking Press, 1965.

Eves, Howard W. *An Introduction to the History of Mathematics*. 6th ed. New York: Saunders College Publishing, 1990.

———. *Great Moments in Mathematics (Before 1650)*. Washington, D.C.: Mathematical Association of America, 1980.

———. *Great Moments in Mathematics (After 1650)*. Washington, D.C.: Mathematical Association of America, 1983.

———. *In Mathematical Circles*. Vols. 1 & 2. Boston: Prindle, Weber & Schmidt, Inc., 1969.

———. *Mathematical Circles Adieu*. Boston: Prindle, Weber & Schmidt, Inc., 1977.

———. *Mathematical Circles Revisited*. Boston: Prindle, Weber & Schmidt, Inc., 1971.

———. *Mathematical Circles Squared*. Boston: Prindle, Weber & Schmidt, Inc., 1972.

Grinstein, Louise S. and Paul J. Campbell. *Women of Mathematics: A Biobibliographic Sourcebook*. New York: Greenwood Press, 1987.

Hooper, Alfred. *Makers of Mathematics*. New York: Random House, 1948.

Infeld, Leopold. *Whom the Gods Love*. Reston, Va.: National Council of Teachers of Mathematics, 1978.

Kramer, Edna E. *The Main Stream of Mathematics*. Greenwich, Conn.: Fawcett, 1961.

————. *The Nature and Growth of Modern Mathematics*. Princeton: Princeton University Press, 1981.

Newman, James R. *The World of Mathematics*. New York: Simon & Schuster, 1956.

Osen, Lynn M. *Women in Mathematics*. Cambridge, Mass.: MIT Press, 1974.

Perl, Teri. *Math Equals: Biographies of Women Mathematicians*. Menlo Park, Ca.: Addison-Wesley, 1978.

Rosen, Sidney. *Galileo and the Magic Numbers*. Boston: Little, Brown & Co., 1958.

Scott, J. F. *A History of Mathematics*. Totowa, N.J.: Barnes and Noble, 1975.

Smith, D. E. *History of Mathematics*. New York: Dover Publications, Inc., 1953.

Sootin, Harry. *Isaac Newton*. New York: Julian Messer, Inc., 1955.

Stonaker, Frances Benson. *Famous Mathematicians*. New York: J.B. Lippincott, 1966.

Struik, Dirk J. *A Concise History of Mathematics*. 4th ed. New York: Dover, Inc., 1987.

Turnbull, Herbert W. *The Great Mathematicians*. New York: New York University Press, 1961.

Wilson, Grove. *Great Men of Science*. Garden City, N.Y.: Garden City, Inc., 1929.

Glossary

◆

abstract rings
A set with two operations (such as addition and multiplication) that has a number of special properties. Studied in abstract algebra.

algebra
The branch of mathematics that uses special symbols, such as letters, to express relationships among numbers.

antilog
See *logarithm*.

astrolabe
An instrument formerly used for finding the altitudes of planets and stars. It was replaced by the sextant.

astronomy
The science that deals with the universe, including stars, planets, and other bodies in space.

atmospheric pressure
Pressure due to the air's weight. Atmospheric pressure on the earth's surface at sea level is about 15 pounds per square inch.

binomial
An algebraic expression consisting of two terms joined by a plus or minus sign. *A+B* is a binomial.

buoyancy
The tendency or ability to keep afloat.

calculus
The branch of mathematics that deals with rates of change such as velocity and acceleration, maximums and minimums, areas, volumes, and many other related subjects.

celestial mechanics
The branch of science concerned with how bodies such as stars and planets move in space.

centimeter
A unit of length in the metric system. A centimeter is equal to one-hundredth of a meter, or approximately .39 of an inch—about the width of a piece of chalk.

circumference
The distance around a circle.

compass
An instrument for drawing circles or measuring distances. A compass is made of two arms joined together at the top.

convergent series
A series is said to converge if the sum of the first n terms approaches a number as n, the number of terms, increases indefinitely. For example, the series $\frac{1}{1} + \frac{1}{2} + \frac{1}{4} + \frac{1}{8} + \frac{1}{16} \cdots$ is convergent since the sum is approaching the number 2.

cycloid
The curve traced by a point on a circle as the circle rolls along a straight line.

diameter
A line segment whose endpoints are on a circle and that passes through the center.

decimeter
A unit of length in the metric system. A decimeter is equal to one-tenth of a meter, or approximately 3.937 inches.

eclipse
The apparent dimming or elimination of light from one planet or celestial body caused when another body passes in front of it.

equation
A statement saying that two expressions are equal.

exponent
In 4^3, 3 is the exponent. It tells that 4 is to be used as a factor three times. It is read "four to the third power."
$$4^3 = 4 \times 4 \times 4 = 64$$

formula
A general rule stated in mathematical language.

geometry
The branch of mathematics that deals with shape, size, and other properties of figures.

gravity
The force that pulls things towards the center of the earth. Gravity is the force that causes objects to fall when they are dropped.

hypotenuse
The side opposite the right angle in a right triangle (a triangle with a right, or 90° angle). The hypotenuse is the longest side.

ideal theory
Deals with mathematical systems that satisfy special conditions. It plays a significant role in number theory.

integer
Any positive or negative whole number or zero. The following are examples of integers: -32, 16, 0, 2001.

irrational number
A number that cannot be expressed as a fraction of *integers*, such as the square root of 2 ($\sqrt{2}$) or pi (π).

isoperimetric figures
Figures having equal *perimeters*.

lever
A rod or bar used to lift things or pry things open.

logarithm or **log**
The logarithm of a number is the exponent when the number is written as a power of a fixed number, called the base. The logarithm of 100 using 10 as the base is 2 since $10^2 = 100$. It is written $\log_{10} 100 = 2$. Used to reduce multiplication to addition (widely used to simplify multiplication before calculators were introduced).

The **antilog** of a number is the number corresponding to a given logarithm. It is written $\text{antilog}_{10} 2 = 100$.

meridian
A circle drawn from any point on the earth's surface and passing through both poles.

meter
The basic unit of length in the metric system. A meter is approximately 39.37 inches, slightly more than one yard.

number theory
The study of the properties of the *integers*, especially concerning factoring, dividing, prime numbers, and related subjects.

optics
The study of light and vision.

partition
The number of partitions of a positive integer is the number of ways it can be written as the sum of positive integers. The number itself is included in this count. The number 4 has 5 partitions, namely $1 + 3, 1 + 1 + 2, 1 + 1 + 1 + 1, 2 + 2$, and 4.

Pascal's triangle
A triangular array of numbers created by beginning and ending each row with 1. Every other number is obtained by adding the two numbers in the preceding row closest to it:

$$
\begin{array}{c}
1 \\
1 \quad 1 \\
1 \quad 2 \quad 1 \\
1 \quad 3 \quad 3 \quad 1 \\
1 \quad 4 \quad 6 \quad 4 \quad 1 \\
1 \quad 5 \quad 10 \quad 10 \quad 5 \quad 1 \\
1 \quad 6 \quad 15 \quad 20 \quad 15 \quad 6 \quad 1
\end{array}
$$

perimeter
The distance around a closed figure. For example, the perimeter of a triangle is the sum of the lengths of the three sides.

pi (π)
The ratio of the *circumference* of a circle to its *diameter*. Approximately equal to 3.14.

Glossary

planisphere
A depiction of space on a chart, showing which stars are visible at a given time.

polygon
A closed figure made up of line segments.

polyhedron
A solid bounded by plane faces.

proof
The logical argument that establishes the truth of a statement.

proportion
A statement that two ratios are equal, such as

$$\frac{3}{6} = \frac{5}{10}$$

Pythagorean theorem
In any right triangle, the square of the length of the *hypotenuse* is equal to the sum of the squares of the lengths of the other sides. If c is the length of the hypotenuse and a and b are the lengths of the other sides, then

$$c^2 = a^2 + b^2$$

ratio
A comparison of two numbers. 3/4 and 3:4 are symbols of the ratio "3 compared to 4."

square root
A number that, when multiplied by itself, will produce a certain number. Since 6 x 6 = 36, 6 is the square root of 36.

theorem
A mathematical statement that has been proved.

topology
That branch of geometry that studies the properties of figures as they are bent, stretched, or otherwise distorted without tearing. Topology has been described as "rubber-sheet" *geometry*.

trigonometry
Historically, the branch of mathematics that deals with the relations of the sides and angles of triangles.

universal gravitation, law of
The theory that there is a pulling attraction between every pair of objects, inversely proportional to the square of the distance between them. Newton discovered this principle in 1687.

vacuum
A space that is completely empty of matter, including air and other gases.

vertex
The corner points of a *polygon* or *polyhedron*.

vertices
Plural of *vertex*.

DATE DUE

Library Store #47-0108 Peel Off Pressure Sensitive